GAINES S. DOBBINS

PIONEER IN RELIGIOUS EDUCATION

AUSTIN C. DOBBINS

BROADMAN PRESS
Nashville, Tennessee

4265-61
ISBN: 0-8054-6561-8

Quotations from:

Gaines S. Dobbins, *Zest for Living* copyright © 1977. Used by permission of Word Books, Publisher, Waco, TX.

E. Y. Mullins, *Why Is Christianity True?* copyright © 1905. Used by permission of Judson Press, Valley Forge, PA.

George Albert Coe, *What is Christian Education?* copyright © 1929. Used by permission of Charles Scribner's Sons, New York, NY.

Ordway Tead, *The Art of Leadership* copyright © 1935. Used by permission of McGraw-Hill Book Co., New York, NY.

Materials published by Broadman Press, Convention Press, and The Sunday School Board, Southern Baptist Convention, Nashville, TN, used by permission.

This book has been styled according to the publisher's guidelines.
Dewey Decimal Classification: B
Subject heading: DOBBINS, GAINES STANLEY
Library of Congress Catalog Card Number: 80-69520
Printed in the United States of America

CONTENTS

Foreword

It is an interesting experience to try to write a word of introduction to a very interesting volume about an extraordinary man. I first met him when the author of this book and I were college classmates at Mississippi College in 1940-41. I knew Dr. Gaines S. Dobbins on a casual level until the early 1960s. Later, our acquaintance was on a much more personal level. One could not be with Gaines Dobbins very long before recognizing the extraordinary quality of the man. His dynamic mind, his wide-ranging interests, his very physical energy, and his irrepressible need to teach immediately made him stand out in anyone's mind.

At the beginning of Dr. Dobbins' ministry, religious education was almost unknown in its present form. He was indeed a pioneer in this field. Religious education largely existed as Sunday School work and sometimes BYPU work. Church administration as a discipline was unknown. When he was called to Southern Seminary to "inaugurate the new Department of Practical Studies at the Seminary," he was asked to add to Sunday School work studies related to "the efficient church." In typical Dobbins style, he soon came to the conclusion that he did not know enough about his subject. In spite of his attempt to resign, the president of the seminary insisted that he remain and that he would have a fruitful ministry at the seminary. Also in typical Dobbins style, he set out to gain an overall view of the field which had been, in effect, chosen for him. More than any other man he structured Southern Baptists' understanding of church administration. He was responsible in many ways for establishing the status that his field presently enjoys in our denomination.

I think it is accurate to say that Dr. Dobbins developed the intellectual underpinnings for the discipline of church administration in theological education. Not only did he produce the first substantial literature on the subject but he also encouraged an almost unlimited number of others to help develop the concept and to give their lives to assisting the churches in developing orderly processes for doing this work.

All of this came out of the fact that Dr. Dobbins was a careful student of the Scripture. It was out of the biblical base of the Great Commission—"teaching them to observe all things whatsoever I have commanded you: and, lo, I am with you alway, even unto the end of the world"—that he developed a rationale for much of the modern understanding of religious education and church administration. His faith in Scripture was unswerving; perhaps it was strengthened by his early agnosticism that had taught him to question almost everything. When he was convinced at last of the total reliability of Scripture and that it was the inspired Word of God, it became the intellectual as well as spiritual base for his life and for his writing.

Dobbins' work was always church oriented. His exegesis of ideas was sharp, crisp, candid, practical, and always aimed at teaching and building. He almost literally brought into existence disciplines that had been ignored or neglected in the broad spectrum of theological education prior to this time. Before his death, he came to see Southern Baptist life and many other denominations saturated with the ideas, concepts, methods, and understandings that he pioneered. In retrospect it is absolutely remarkable that one man could encompass so broad an area of intellectual pursuit, be so prolific in the exposition of his ideas for the practical utilization of others, and at the same time remain a thoroughgoing student.

Dr. Dobbins made several great contributions to Christian life. One of these was that through the development of modern understandings of the meaning of the Great Commission he brought richness to the life of the local congregation that had never been achieved to that point. With these ideas he built into the fabric of the church the exercise of the priesthood of the individual believer and pointed out that accountability and responsibility for ministry is a portion of the life of every believer. This is no mean accomplishment.

Between 1916 and 1978 he wrote more than 4,900 articles for publications of all descriptions and thirty-three books. During this time, he was constantly involved in preaching and teaching, as well as his writing activities.

The relationship of Dr. Dobbins with the Sunday School Board was a close and fruitful one. In 1919, at the urging of the Southern Baptist Convention, an editorial department was developed at the Board. Dr. Dobbins, who continued his editorship of *Home and Foreign Fields,* was part of a four-man editorial council, along with Hight C Moore, E. C. Dargan, and Landrum P. Leavell. Dr. Dobbins' service to the Sunday School Board spanned more than the four years he was an employee (1916-1920). Not only did he edit *Home and Foreign Fields* until 1932 but through his writing and his counsel he continued to influence Board literature until his death.

In my own personal relationships with Dr. Dobbins across the years, I found that he was always courteous, refined, and he never ceased teaching. I watched him closely in his second teaching career at Golden Gate Baptist Theological Seminary and found him making an enormous contribution, not only to the students who passed that way but to the entire west coast of the United States. Whenever we were working together on committees or serving on the same platform or simply visiting together, Dobbins was always busy trying to expose me to new ideas, new concepts, or something that he was particularly interested in at the time. This continued even after I became president of the Baptist Sunday School Board. My last contact with Dr. Dobbins, prior to his promotion to glory, was as he worked on a book related to Bold Mission Thrust, the present involvement of the Southern Baptist Convention.

It is a pleasure for me to commend to you this volume concerning Dr. Dobbins' life and work for his Master. You will find in it a great deal of the man himself together with his spirit. You will find in it the careful, scholarly competence of his son, my lifelong friend, Dr. Austin C. Dobbins.

GRADY C. COTHEN

Preface

Why should anyone be interested in a biography of Gaines S. Dobbins? I am fascinated by his life, but as his biographer and son I may be regarded as being prejudiced.

Thirteen million Southern Baptists might suggest a better reason. Phrases such as "Southern Baptists' greatest teacher of Religious Education" (Charles Carter), "Southern Baptists' most honored and respected leader in the field of Church Administration" (Allen W. Graves), and "the most prolific writer in Southern Baptist history" (Erwin L. McDonald) indicate the respect and love given to Dr. Dobbins by his denomination. As "Mr. Religious Education," "Mr. Church Administration," and "Mr. Southern Baptist," for 69 years (1909-1978), Dr. Dobbins both reflected and guided the events which have shaped Southern Baptist history.

A third answer may be suggested. Dr. Dobbins' life is the story of a boy who was born on a farm and moved to the city where he became a "success" at the age of sixteen. And so he earned millions and became president of a large corporation? No, although this might have been the story of his life. As a boy, Gaines Dobbins was a thoroughgoing materialist, even an agnostic. But he discovered that materialism leads to a dead end—just as many executives have discovered today, too late. The story of Dr. Dobbins' life, then, is the story of a pilgrimage which led an intelligent but rebellious young boy from a worldly definition of success to a goal of living for Christ as the only means by which success can be achieved in this world.

Gaines S. Dobbins: Pioneer in Religious Education is not a conventional biography. If it has any antecedents, its type is Wordsworth's "Prelude," a spiritual biography. A deeply religious man, Dr. Dobbins was convinced that Christianity is more than a creed or a set of doctrines. Rather it is the living expression of the means by which each individual may reach his or her highest potential. "Regeneration" and "salvation" perhaps are old-fashioned terms. Yet they express Dr. Dobbins' point of view precisely. To each individual Christ promises and provides—if his claims are accepted—life and life-changing experiences.

Three collections of materials pertaining to Dr. Dobbins' career exist in (1) The Southern Baptist Theological Seminary Library, Louisville, (2) the Dargan-Carver Library, Nashville, and (3) presently in the home of the biographer in Birmingham. Included in the latter collection is a full bibliography of his writings. Dr. Dobbins left three autobiographical typescripts (8, 6, and 19 pages), each undated, of his life. These are listed as Biography I, II, and III. Aside from these sources, autobiographical tapes recorded by Virginia Howell and Betsy Fleenor, his granddaughters, Elmer L. Gray, Badgett Dillard, K. Stephen Combs, and Andrew B. Rawls, as well as 45 articles written for *The Alabama Baptist* from 1968-78, furnish the major sources for the biography. Portions of the study appeared earlier in the *Review and Expositor,* July 1978.

For assistance in obtaining materials and checking facts, I am deeply indebted to Badgett Dillard, Vice-President for Business Affairs, Southern Seminary, Louisville; Allen W. Graves, Dean, School of Religious Education, Southern; Ronald F. Deering, Librarian, and Paul M. Debusman, Reference and Serials Librarian, Southern; Wayne E. Oates, Professor of Psychiatry and Behavioral Science, School of Medicine, University of Louisville; Harold K. Graves, President Emeritus, Golden Gate Seminary, Mill Valley, California; Mrs. C. P. Campbell, Church Clerk, Pachuta Baptist Church; Mayor and Mrs. L. C. Rhoden, Pachuta, Mississippi; Alice G. Cox, Librarian, Mississippi Baptist Historical Commission, Clinton; Brooks H. Wester, Pastor, First Baptist Church, Hattiesburg; Wayne G. Berry, Pastor, Galilee First Baptist Church, Gloster; members of Dr. Dobbins' early pastorate at New Albany; Howard Gallimore, Supervisor, Dargan-Carver Library; Lynn E. May, Executive Director-Treasurer, Southern Baptist Historical Commission, Nashville; Margaret Peterson, Librarian, Home Mission Board, Atlanta; Nancy Nell Stanley, Librarian, Jenkins Library and Archives, Foreign Mission Board, Richmond; Charles Carter, Pastor, Shades Mountain Baptist Church, Birmingham; Ruric Wheeler, Vice-

President for Academic Affairs, Elizabeth Wells, Special Collections Librarian, Samford University, Birmingham; Doris De Vault, Coordinator of Special Services, Woman's Missionary Union, Birmingham; Hudson Baggett, Editor, *The Alabama Baptist,* Birmingham; and many other friends.

A separate sentence should be devoted to my wife—without whose love, patience, and understanding this biography could not have been written.

AUSTIN C. DOBBINS

1
Beginnings

Gaines Stanley Dobbins was born July 29, 1886, on his grandparents' farm near Langsdale, a sparsely populated farming community in Clark(e) County, Mississippi. In 1887, Gaines' parents, Charles and Letitia Dobbins, moved with their seven children from Langsdale to a farm near Pachuta, a village some twenty miles northwest of Langsdale. The reason for their change of residence was largely economic. In 1886-87, Ezekiel and Mary Dobbins, Charles' parents, owned two farms, one consisting of 354 acres near Langsdale, the other of 228 acres near Pachuta. Langsdale was a sleepy post hamlet with a population of less than fifty. In contrast, with a population of 500, Pachuta was a thriving trading center with a sawmill, a gin, seven to eight stores, a school, and two churches. The sawmill offered opportunities of employment unavailable in Langsdale. Moreover, located on the newly built New Orleans and Northeastern Railroad, Pachuta offered direct connections with Hattiesburg and Meridian.

For a farm family, living close to a railroad was advantageous. Cotton requires transportation. In 1887 there were few (if any) paved roads in Mississippi. Payment for transportation over muddy, frequently impassable roads generally required a sixth of the sales price of the staple. In an economy in which $300 a year represented good wages, a saving of $50 was enough to justify moving from one location to another.

To a modern reader, $50 does not sound like much money. During the second half of the nineteenth century, however, in Mississippi times were hard. Money was difficult to obtain. Between 1887-93, cotton, the only crop on which money could be borrowed, sold for eight cents a pound, only slightly more than it cost to grow. Interest rates were high (10 percent for 5 months). Fortunately, it did not take much money to operate a farm. Cotton seed could be used for fertilizer. Clothes were homemade. Money was required to pay for schooling, taxes, and hired help, but wages could be "paid" by providing meals and sharing a percentage of the crop with the laborers.

It was in this type of environment that Gaines Dobbins grew up. His parents and grandparents were farmers. Charles Wesley (1850-1910), Gaines' father, was the second son of Ezekiel (Ezekel) Stanley and Mary Wimbish Dobbins, moderately well-to-do farmers from Langsdale and Pachuta. Ezekiel was the son of William Dobbins, a schoolteacher, and Nancy Stanley, daughter of Ezekiel Stanley, a prosperous farmer from Covington, Georgia. Nancy's brother, a Methodist minister, Dr. Thomas Stanley, helped to found Emory College (Emory University). Letitia Gaines (1849-1940), Gaines' mother, was the third daughter of Philip Pendleton and Rebecca Pippin Gaines, who owned a large farm in Choctaw County (near Gilberton), Alabama. Philip was the son of James Strother Gaines, a Virginia farmer, and nephew of General Edmund Pendleton Gaines, an outstanding figure in the War of 1812. Traditionally the Stanleys and Gaines were educators, ministers, soldiers, physicians, lawyers—professional men. ("The Stanleys, sir, take to professional life, at least in North Carolina, sir.") In Alabama and Mississippi, however, during the post-Civil War period, their offspring generally were farmers who were land-poor, raised cotton, and struggled to exist.

In 1887 Charles and Letitia Dobbins were farmers who, like their parents, possessed land but had little money. Cotton prices were low. But then no one else in the neighborhood had much money either. In Pachuta, times were hard but life was good. The land was productive, and Charles was a skillful farmer. The Dobbins' home, composed of three bedrooms, a parlor, an attic or loft for the boys, with a kitchen separated from the house (as was usual), was a better-than-average farmer's house. In this setting Gaines (or "Bud," his family nickname) learned to work, to share what he had, and to do without whatever was beyond his reach. He helped his father and his elder brother, Austin, tend the cattle, slop the hogs, feed the chickens, take care of the chores which farm boys long have been accustomed to perform. Most of the farm labor was performed by "hired" help (freedmen) and the older members of the family. Occasionally, however, even Gaines was required to work in the fields. Chopping cotton, he discovered, is hard work. All in all, however, though he had few material advantages, Gaines had a happy childhood. He enjoyed his special task, currying the horses, Mike and Nellie. And he found that living in the loft with Austin was fun.

Occasionally, of course, he faced difficulties. He made the mistake of using Sloans Liniment to soothe his chafed skin after Nellie, who had run away while he was riding her, finally brought him home. To Gaines, turpentine (Sloans Liniment) was not a satisfactory emollient. Again, he was not allowed to attend school until he was seven. Grade school was four miles away, a distance too far for Gaines to walk alone until he was older. Taught reading, spelling, and numbers at home by his mother, he expected to be placed in the second grade when he entered school. Tested by his teacher, a disciplinarian who believed in education by the rule, he did well in reading and spelling. But he knew his multiplication tables only through the nines, not through the twelves. Threatened with disgrace (demotion to the first grade), he followed his mother around the house over the weekend, repeating the tables until he knew them by heart. On Monday, frightened but determined, he satisfied the teacher's requirements for entrance into the second grade.

Church attendance also caused minor problems. Charles Wesley was a Methodist. Letitia, who found no authority in the Bible, she said, for the christening of infants, was a Baptist. Gaines' early church orientation, therefore, was both Methodist and Baptist. Actually, he said, there wasn't much difference between the two churches. Both were barn-like, one-room buildings. Perhaps the Baptist facilities were the more attractive. In the Baptist church "the pews were more comfortable, the room was larger, boys and girls of kindergarten age met separately on seats in the back of the church." In the Methodist church, where the Sunday School also met in the back of the auditorium, the pupils sat on planks laid across risers. "On the first seat were the little fellows, under five years; on the next, children from about five to seven; on the top level were the older boys and girls, ranging from about eight to twelve." What was he taught? "I haven't the slightest notion," Dr. Dobbins commented later. "Apparently the teacher's main occupation was trying to keep us quiet!" (*Search*, Winter 1975).

As a young boy, Gaines' impressions of school and church were not altogether favorable. He was amenable to discipline, but he did not enjoy the restrictions which were placed upon him by his mentors. However, the school term lasted only seven months. Even church attendance had its good points, for church meant going somewhere, and on Sundays he was allowed to hitch up Mike and Nellie and drive the family wagon to Pachuta. Except for minor difficulties, as a boy Gaines found that life was good.

Then, in 1891-92, disaster struck. First, while loading a bale of cotton, Charles injured his back, making it difficult for him to farm. Next, Austin, who was working in Pachuta to earn money to enter Millsaps College, was killed in a railroad accident. Ordinarily Austin worked at the local station as a telegrapher/dispatcher. In an emergency he had agreed to serve as a brakeman on the run to Meridian. While Austin was coupling the cars, the engineer moved the train—some said he had been drinking—and Austin was crushed beneath the wheels. Without adequate medical attention, a week before Christmas, he died. Gaines had idolized his brother. "Why?" he asked repeatedly. "Why did God let Austin die?" Austin had planned to become a Methodist minister, to serve God. Yet at the age of seventeen he had been killed. Why? *(The Alabama Baptist,* Oct. 9, 1969.) The incident marked Gaines' later life, for, try as they might, his parents were unable to console him. Finally, a third disaster. Charles lost his crop. He had sold his cotton, the family's "cash crop," to a Hattiesburg factor who defaulted (yet he was a "pillar of the church"), leaving Charles unable to pay his debts. From 1892-94, almost penniless, the Dobbins' remained near Pachuta, operating a commissary-chuck type of wagon for the lumbermen as they moved from tract to tract in Clark and Jasper counties. They had done this earlier, supplementing their income from farming. But conditions worsened. In 1893 the country suffered a severe depression; in 1894 the price of cotton fell below five cents a pound.

In 1895, traveling by wagon, the Dobbins' left Pachuta for Hattiesburg, a town that offered fairer prospects. Hattiesburg had a population of almost 3,500. Charles' health had improved, but he still could not perform hard labor. Perhaps he could make a living working in one of the fifty-nine lumber mills located in the Hattiesburg area. Surrounded with timber worth at least $200 million, in 1895 Hattiesburg was a boom town which offered wages of a dollar a day, twice the amount offered farm laborers. Instead, on the outskirts of Hattiesburg, Charles rented a ten-acre plot. Gaines, now "going on ten," became a door-to-door salesman, before breakfast peddling vegetables, turnips (three bunches for ten cents), butter (twenty cents a pound), and eggs (twenty-five cents for two dozen) from his father's farm. Later, for $2.50 a week, he worked as a grocery clerk and delivery boy. His earnings usually were placed in the family account, but this made little difference. The Dobbins' always shared what they had.

Then Charles had a better idea. Too many Hattiesburg citizens had gardens for truck farming to be profitable, but Hattiesburg lacked a hotel. On West Pine Street, a two-story house with a large loft was available for rent. Why not use the loft for lodging and furnish food from the farm at fifty cents a day ($2.50 a week) to accommodate the large number of potential lodgers who had crowded into the city to work in the lumber mills? Cots (10 to 20) placed together as close as possible would provide adequate sleeping arrangements. The boys, Gaines, Vivian, and Earl, could work on the farm. The girls, Corinne, Cecilia, Nettie, and Virginia, could manage the boardinghouse. This was a type of work with which the Dobbins' were familiar. Wealth might not be the result, but they could earn a comfortable living.

The decision of his parents to operate a boardinghouse (later the Dobbins Hotel) made a crucial difference in Gaines' life. Here he became acquainted with mill hands, printers, electricians, actors, baseball players, railroad workers, the many types of persons, all different, who became "guests" in his home. Since the mill workers had to be at work by six in the morning, the "hosts" rose at 4:30, when the whistle blew, in order to serve breakfast, pack the lunch boxes, and get the men to work on time. One of the boarders, an Englishman, a former magazine editor who had made his way to Hattiesburg, became interested in the hotel keeper's son. Largely through his influence, Gaines became acquainted with good literature—*Ivanhoe, Oliver Twist, David Copperfield*—instead of the five-cent Frank Merriwell and Diamond Dick type of novels which, much to his mother's dismay, he had begun to read. To his amazement, he discovered that the books recommended by the Englishman were more interesting than the "trash" (his mother's term) he had been reading. A second boarder, a Civil War veteran named Colonel H. S. Evans, was editor of *The Hattiesburg Progress,* a weekly printed at the shop where he worked. Colonel Evans secured employment for Gaines as office boy and printer's apprentice. Thus, at the age of twelve, Gaines gave up his occupation as a grocery clerk to become a journalist.

At the printing office—"doing anything that no one else wanted to do"—Gaines ran errands, swept the floor, and picked up the type that had been dropped. He learned to set type and to operate the Martha Washington hand press: Position the paper (one sheet at a time), put on a fly and let down, fold under and press the lever, take out the paper and lay it aside. One day, he recalled, a mischievous printer asked him if he wanted to see some "type lice." "Look carefully," he urged. "Put your head close to the type." Then, pressing the separated sections of the type together suddenly, the printer squirted inky water over Gaines' face (Biography II, *c.*1955). The workers at the printing office were scarcely the kindest of men. However, continuing his interest in Gaines, Colonel Evans required his protégé to keep a record of all the words in the day's copy which he could not define. "The measure of a man's intelligence," he insisted, "is his ability to use words wisely." At the close of the day's work Gaines had to look up the unfamiliar words in the big dictionary in Colonel Evans' office. Any word he had misspelled he was required to correct in the galleys on his own time (Biography I, *c.*1950).

Later, encouraged by Colonel Evans and W. H. Seitzler, owner of *The Progress,* Gaines began writing squibs about the guests at his parents' hotel. One of his squibs (or notices) concerned a third boarder, a Mr. Bradley, an electrician who offered Gaines a job as night operator on the recently established (100 manual) Hattiesburg telephone exchange. Although he already was working in the afternoons after school, Gaines accepted the additional work gladly. The shift as operator involved duty from 7 PM to 7 AM, but work as an operator was more interesting than working at home. At home (the hotel) each morning he brought in the firewood, started the kitchen fire, and, before leaving for school, took care of the horses. In the afternoons he worked on the farm or performed chores at the hotel. The prospect of avoiding routine as well as adding $5.00 a week salary to the $3.50 he was earning at the printing office was too enticing to resist. No child labor laws existed to prevent him from accepting the offer, and his family needed the money. Combining work with sleep and study, Gaines contrived an alarm clock device which awakened him when he was needed as an operator. As a result he received pay whether he worked, studied, or slept. There was another reward. Answering calls and listening to conversations, he said, enabled him to learn more about human nature and the "goings-on" of a small town than he could ever have learned from books!

At the age of twelve Gaines was a printer's devil. At the age of fourteen he was an experienced typesetter and reporter. At the age of sixteen, disillusioned with education, he decided to quit school to become a full-time journalist. As a future editor of a big city newspaper, what need did he have for further education? Woodson, Vardaman, Patten, Ochs, Harris, Durkin, Clemens—the list of formally uneducated but ambitious boys who became successful nineteenth-century editors is extensive. Under the tutelage of Colonel Evans, his unnamed friend (the Englishman), and his high-school teachers, Miss Croyzette Watkins and Mr. F. B. Woodley, he felt that already he had read more than most college students when they completed their courses. And quite possibly he had. He read so extensively that, he said, arousing jealousy among the other students, he became a "sort of source student" for Miss Watkins, his English teacher. A list of the authors whom Gaines is known to have read by the age of sixteen includes such writers as Scott, Dickens, Browning, Clemens, Dunne, Eggleston, Emerson, Hugo, Ingersoll, O. Henry, Paine, Rousseau, Shakespeare, Stevenson, Tennyson, and Tolstoy.

Although incomplete, the list is revealing. In 1902 few high-school teachers would have recommended that teenagers read Rousseau *(Emile)*, Paine *(The Age of Reason)*, or Ingersoll *(Some Mistakes of Moses)*. According to popular belief, Rousseau and Paine were atheists while Ingersoll, at best, was an agnostic. Each regarded Christianity as a force which stifled intellectual progress. Reading of these authors indicates the influence of Colonel Evans, who not only encouraged his protégé to recognize the value of language but also to respect the views of Paine and Ingersoll as well. It is not surprising, then, that in his Junior year in high school Gaines became dissatisfied. Stimulated by Colonel Evans, who hated preachers but loved good whiskey, Gaines sought to combine standards of good literature and journalism with views advocated by Paine and Ingersoll.

Applying these standards to the Bible, he found that Christianity contained beliefs that could not be verified objectively. What proof is there of immortality? (Why had Austin died?) Do honesty and justice actually exist? (How could a moral man, a man who called himself a Christian, defraud his father of the money due him for his crop?) To these questions the church provided answers. To Gaines, as well as to Colonel Evans, Paine, and Ingersoll, the answers were unsatisfactory. "As a reporter," wrote Dr. Dobbins in *Great Teachers Make a Difference* (1965),

> I knew . . . that some of the leading churchmen were falsifying their tax returns. One man, prominent in his church, owned squalid rental property in the "Negro quarters" on which he boasted of a 20 per cent net return. The courts and law enforcement officers practiced unconcealed discrimination against "niggers" and "poor whites," notwithstanding church affiliation on the part of judges and police.

Even *The Progress*, the paper for which he worked, was "a newspaper written solely for whites." Apparently Paine and Ingersoll were right: Enlightened self-interest is the first law of nature.

Brilliant, independent, rebellious (as teenagers frequently are), from 1900 to 1906 Gaines regarded himself an agnostic. Gaines Stanley Dobbins an agnostic? Yes, although deist perhaps is a more suitable term. In the spring of 1906, in a college theme, he stated his position clearly:

> Why strive for an education? Why study and try to maintain some degree of health? Primarily I suspect my motivation is of a wholly selfish origin. I wish to be a success in some line of work, chiefly for my own satisfaction and pleasure. Secondly, I feel it is a duty to my family to succeed because in so doing it will afford them pleasure as well as me, and because I feel that if I ever have a family they should believe the same, ultimately again giving me pleasure. Thirdly, I believe I live and struggle because I have some vague intuitive idea that thought and knowledge have some definite connection with the mighty forces behind the universe.

Disillusioned with his community, nevertheless Gaines sought to be a positive force, an impartial observer who would report the facts, indulge in investigative reporting ("muckraking") perhaps at times, but at all times maintain standards of fair-mindedness and honesty.

It was at this point in Gaines' career that Providence (was it Providence?) again took a hand. In 1901 the Finkbine Lumber Company, one of the largest sawmill operating companies in the Hattiesburg area, announced plans to build a lumber mill at McHenry, a village located midway between Hattiesburg and Gulfport. Here a modern hotel was built to house the anticipated influx of laborers. In June 1902, accepting the position of hotel manager, Charles Dobbins moved his family to McHenry. Unfortunately, for various reasons the mill was located at Wiggins, a village ten miles distant from McHenry. Since hotel-keeping at McHenry was unprofitable, disappointed, Charles returned to Hattiesburg with his family in September to resume boarding house operations on East Pine Street. However, since he had found employment on the local newspaper *(The Star)*, Gaines remained in McHenry.

For Gaines the decision to remain in McHenry was not wholly voluntary. In fact, it was the result of a disaster. On Saturday, September 6, two weeks before he was scheduled to return to Hattiesburg, at the print shop Gaines dropped a page form of legal notices (one fourth of the newspaper), pieing the type on the floor. Understandably upset, Mr. Oscar Grace, his employer, insisted that Gaines remain in McHenry until he had distributed and reset the type. It was during this time that Gaines became acquainted with Lucius L. Patterson, the recently appointed principal of the McHenry High School.

The meeting was significant, for Professor Patterson (later Dean of Engineering at Mississippi State), challenged Gaines' concepts of education. True, he agreed, Gaines' intellectual horizons possibly were wider than those of many college students. But his reading had been desultory, lacking in balance, a basic requirement in education. Professor Patterson, who had only one student in his Senior class, proposed that Gaines remain in McHenry, support himself by continuing to work as a printer, and finish his high school education. He would have to pay tuition, but Professor Patterson's salary would remain the same. The suggestion startled Gaines, for it was contrary to his view of human nature. Self-interest, he had been taught, was the basic rule of life. Yet here was a man who proposed—unselfishly proposed—to teach composition, literature, mathematics, Latin, and Greek, a course not ordinarily offered in high school, without additional pay. Moreover, although he had earned two degrees, Professor Patterson regarded education as a goal which never could be completed. As an engineer he should have been skeptical of the value of a classical education. Instead he regarded Latin and Greek as keys to knowledge. Amazing! Gaines knew little mathematics and no Greek. Recognizing the opportunity Mr. Patterson offered him, Gaines decided to remain in McHenry to obtain his high school diploma. His parents might have objected, for Gaines had just turned sixteen, but his mother and Corinne, his eldest sister, wanted him to continue his education. Had he returned to Hattiesburg he might have dropped out of school.

In 1977, in *Zest for Living,* Dr. Dobbins recalled his experiences as a high-school Senior:

> With just two of us in the class, if there was any reciting or research or writing, we had to do it. [Mark Hopkins on one end of the log, two students on the other!] Our teacher was expert in math, my weakest subject but the girl's strongest. The course in English was almost on a college level—my strongest subject, the girl's weakest. Ethel did better in Latin. I prided myself in going ahead of her in Greek.

Presenting a view quite different from that of Paine and Ingersoll, Professor Patterson challenged Gaines' assumptions in three areas: (1) He maintained that education consists of more than facts. (2) He regarded education as a life activity. Conclusions are not always valid at the age of sixteen. (3) He believed that success in life involves more than selfishly achieving one's goals. "Make good wherever you are," he said. Success involves serving God and living for others regardless of one's position. To Gaines these concepts scarcely were new. They were principles which he had been taught at home, in Sunday School, and in church. But now they were enforced by the influence of unselfish example. Who, then, was right, Patterson or Paine, Paine or Patterson?

Puzzled, but still rebellious, in May 1903, Gaines returned to Hattiesburg to become a full-time journalist. Under A. J. ("Cyclone Jim") Haynie, the new editor-owner of *The Progress,* his abilities were recognized almost immediately. For not only was Gaines a capable worker (a Master Printer) but he was also reliable. He did not drink. The other printers did, heavily. Newspaper publication, difficult at best, becomes impossible with unreliable printers. In July Gaines was made foreman of the print shop. In August he was promoted to the rank of chief reporter. In September he became city editor and Associated Press Correspondent for South Mississippi as well. By November *The Progress* had grown from four to twelve pages with "advertising matter double that of any other paper in the state." Then, in December, apparently attracted by a higher salary, Gaines resigned from *The Progress* to become shop foreman for his brother-in-law, Sam Martin, owner of the Martin Printing Company, the largest job printing shop in Hattiesburg.

In June the major reason for Gaines' change of positions became evident, for, on June 21, six months after he had left *The Progress,* although only seventeen he became coeditor (later editor and, from November through May, proprietor) of *The Saturday Evening Eye,* a newly established newsmagazine published by the Martin Printing Company. (The story of Gaines' activities rivals the plot of a Frank Merriwell novel!) Within three months, with 500 paid subscribers and "street sales in addition," *The Eye* had become the second largest weekly in Mississippi. Published at five cents a copy, a typical issue contained two cover pages, three pages of editorials, six pages of feature articles, news reports, fillers ("Eyelets"), legal notices, and seven to nine pages of advertisements (at $10 a page? In 1903 *The Progress* charged 5 cents a line.).

Financially *The Eye* was a success. Since he was attempting to buy the paper, Gaines received little of the profits himself, of course. The profits were reinvested in equipment for the shop, including a Linotype and a Miehle power press. However, for his reporting, the aspect of *The Eye* in which he was particularly interested, Gaines was praised highly by the editors of the Waynesborough *News-Beacon* and the Gulfport *News* (March, May 1905). The editor of the *News-Beacon,* interestingly enough, was his friend Jim Haynie. Even more gratifying, perhaps, was the reaction of the local readers. In Hattiesburg his editorials were well received—read, discussed, commented upon from the pulpit. His most influential article, a blistering account of a Hattiesburg lynching (Aug. 31, 1905), was reprinted in the New Orleans *Picayune.* A second article, an investigative report of the activities of the local bootlegger, almost got Gaines into trouble. Hattiesburg was a "dry" city legally, but liquor was available to all who wanted it. Gaines decided to "print the facts." A few days later, Jim Bullitt, the bootlegger,

> entered the printing office, a huge pistol in his holster, looked about, and demanded to see the editor. Everybody ducked behind a printing case or press and the proprietor ducked out the back door. Gaines was pecking away at the

typewriter, unaware of what was happening. Bullitt walked over to where Gaines was seated and asked, "Did you write that piece about me?" "Y-y-es," Gaines stammered. "Then," said Mr. Bullitt, "here's two dollars. I want to subscribe for your sheet. That was a right good piece" (Biography II, *c.* 1955; apparently no copy of this issue of *The Eye* exists).

As a result Gaines became something of a local hero.

Nevertheless, despite his "fame," Gaines remained dissatisfied. "Superficial success," he wrote in *Zest for Living* (1977),

> left me with a strange feeling of emptiness. My wonderful high school teacher had implanted in me an ideal that went beyond just making good in a newspaper job. With his college and university degrees, he had yet become principal and teacher in a small school on meager salary in a "hick" town. I couldn't get away from his influence.

Thus, although he was an agnostic, Gaines continued to attend Sunday School. In *The Eye*, devoting at least a page each week to the nine local churches, he presented the cause of religion—albeit sometimes caustically. In his editorials he sought to be fair-minded, objective, rational, and factual. Yet the views of *The Eye*, he recognized, were largely ineffectual. The conditions which he reported—Whitecapism, blind tigers, gambling, ineffective laws, incompetent officials, unsanitary holes on Main Street—apparently remained unchanged.

Why? According to Colonel Evans, undesirable conditions could be overcome by persuading men that it was to their advantage to act. Herein lay Gaines' dilemma. If the type of thinking advocated by Colonel Evans was valid, then "truth once known should produce intelligent action." But truth (objective reporting) did not always evoke this response. If the type of thinking represented by Professor Patterson was valid, change required acceptance of goals outside of and higher than those conceived by mankind—but this view, the view of the churches, also raised difficulties. Who was right?

Resigning his position as editor of *The Eye*, in October 1905, Gaines sought to resolve his dilemma by enrolling as a student at Mississippi College, a small Baptist denominational college located at Clinton, a village 100 miles north of Hattiesburg. Through his high-school experience he had enlarged his intellectual horizons. A *college* education should be even more worthwhile.

2
College and Seminary

Why Mississippi College? William Paton Dobbins, his uncle, superintendent of schools at Oxford, had offered to furnish Gaines room and board if he attended the University of Mississippi. Instead he had chosen Mississippi College. Why? This was a question Gaines asked himself repeatedly in November when he arrived in Clinton, a month late because of a yellow fever epidemic which had closed the schools, including Mississippi College.

The delay had allowed him to retain his position in Hattiesburg through December as editor of *The Eye* while he attended classes at Clinton in November, a seeming impossibility. The extra income had been welcome, but now, as he surveyed his new surroundings, his effort seemed questionably worthwhile. In 1905 Clinton was a "shabby little village" with a bank, two or three stores, a girl's school, the college, and little else. A boardwalk that needed repair stretched from the college to the railroad depot. The college itself consisted of four buildings, a "ramshackle" brick chemistry building, two "dilapidated" frame classroom buildings, and an antebellum chapel which still bore shell marks from a skirmish between Confederate and Union soldiers forty years before (Biography III, c.1971; *Clarion-Ledger*, May 16, 1947). It was in these surroundings that Gaines sought an education. Apparently he had made a foolish decision. Why had he selected Mississippi College?

"Almost against my will," Dr. Dobbins stated later, "I was moved to select a Christian school." In part his decision was the result of overpersuasion by Dr. W. T. Lowery, the president of Mississippi College, whose appeal for students on his visit to Hattiesburg the preceding spring had caused Gaines to consider Mississippi College. No less important, indeed much more important, Gaines' decision to enter Mississippi College was the product of forces of which at the time he was unaware. In the spring of 1905, Gaines had become the object of prayer by his friends: Mrs. I. P. Trotter, his Sunday School teacher and wife of the pastor of the First Baptist Church; N. R. McCullough, a deacon at Main Street Baptist Church; J. C. Ballard, cashier of Citizen's Bank; L. L. Patterson, his former teacher; and others. Mrs. Trotter was the wife of a graduate of Mississippi College, Mr. McCullough was a trustee, Mr. Ballard and Mr. Patterson were graduates of the college. Each recognized Gaines' need for the type of Christian influence offered by Mississippi College.

God moves in mysterious ways. Gaines had saved some money, but his salary of $18 a week had not allowed him to save much. His parents could not help him. Sale of *The Eye* to his brother-in-law, Mr. Martin, had not brought him much money, for he had not invested much to begin with. He had planned to attend college—eventually; in 1905, however, he felt that he simply could not afford the cost. Tuition and expenses for four years would require at least $900, a year's salary or enough to buy a quarter section of good land. Mr. Ballard, the banker, supplemented his prayers by offering to deposit $300 to Gaines' account, saying, "You can draw on this sum if you have to. Now you don't have an excuse. Go ahead!" Gaines could earn money working as a printer between sessions. Which college should he attend? "Why, Mississippi College, of course."

Thus in November 1905, on faith, although he regarded himself as an agnostic, Gaines returned to school—

To disappointment. He had made a mistake. "I was in despair. What have I done? This is a despicable place," he recalls saying to himself when he first saw Mississippi College. But Mississippi College was composed of more than buildings. The students—though 60 of the 360 were preachers—were friendly. And the faculty, composed of experienced instructors, were well-trained and understanding. Recognizing that a student with five years of writing experience scarcely needed further training in composition, Dr. P. H. Eager, professor of English, granted Gaines advanced standing (3 units) in English. Similarly, advanced standing (5 units) was approved by Professors J. M. Sharp and J. T. Wallace, the heads of the departments of mathematics and history. To obtain advanced standing in languages (6 units) required passing qualifying examinations in Latin and Greek, examinations which

Gaines knew he could not pass. It had been almost three years since he had studied languages in high school. Yet if he could obtain advanced credit, he could enter college as a Sophomore and graduate in three years!

Tutored by Dr. A. J. Aven ("Ajax"), the head of the department of languages, Gaines passed the examinations. Since this incident led to the most significant experience of his college life, quotation from Dr. Dobbins' recollections in *Zest for Living* and *Great Teachers Make a Difference* seems appropriate:

When I offered to pay Dr. Aven for his services, he said, "I'll make just one charge—I want you to come to my Sunday School class." How could I refuse? . . . Here was a Christian whom I genuinely admired and to whom I was sincerely grateful. Reluctantly I agreed to attend his Sunday School class, but with the inward reservation that I would not let it affect my treasured unbelief *(Zest for Living)*.

The next semester I entered a college class [in Bible] taught by the venerable H. F. Sproles, whose textbook was E. Y. Mullins' *Why Is Christianity True?* I re-examined my skeptical position but remained unconvinced.

That fall a campus-wide revival meeting was held under the guidance of P. I. Lipsey with T. T. Martin as evangelist *(Great Teachers Make a Difference)*. The choir sang, "Where Is My Wandering Boy," and "Just As I Am," and the preacher pictured the joys of heaven and the horrors of hell, pleading with his hearers to claim the one and avoid the other. Frankly, I wasn't impressed *(Zest for Living)*.

Chapel attendance was compulsory; hence, I listened to the morning sermons but doggedly refused to go to the evening services—on grounds that I had to study. My grades were good and I didn't want to risk lowering them. The truth is that I was afraid that I might be convinced against my will and go over to the "Holy Joes," the ministerial students, some of whom I heartily disliked.

It was Wednesday night and interest in the meeting was mounting to a climax. An all-night prayer meeting was held. Somehow I became strangely restless, left my books, and went out on the railroad track behind the boarding house [Mrs. Kethley's], and walked back and forth in the moonlight. I felt desperately unhappy as with myself I argued the case against becoming a Christian and resolutely determined that I was not going to be overpersuaded. I did not know that my name was on the prayer list of those for whom a devoted band of Christians [led by Dr. Aven] were at that moment praying.

The next morning in Latin class an unusual thing happened *(Great Teachers Make a Difference)*. Dr. Aven translated the passage from Cicero, gave the constructions, then dismissed the class. Wondering, we began to leave, when he called my name. . . .

"Gaines," he said, "I'm concerned about you. You're a good student. You have a good mind and high ambition. But none of this will be any good without one thing that you lack."

"What's that?" I inquired.

"You're not a Christian—and that's a fatal mistake."

"But I just don't believe all that a Christian is supposed to believe."

"I understand," he said. "I once had that problem myself. You don't have to agree with everything others believe in order to be a Christian." He handed me a pocket New Testament. "Read John 7:17."

I read aloud. "If any man will do his will, he shall know of the doctrine, whether it be of God, or whether I speak of myself."

"You are science-minded," he continued. "How does a scientist prove that a claim is true or false?"

"Why, by testing it, of course."

"That is what Jesus is challenging you to do! He claims that faith in him will change your life. Try it! Put aside your intellectual difficulties and simply say, 'I will take him at his word, put his claim to the test, read further his claims and promises with open mind, and act on the assumption that he is who he claims to be and will do what he promises to do' " *(Zest for Living)*.

Test the claims of Christ. Begin with the major premise; then go from the minor premise to the conclusion. "But I can't believe all that the preacher preaches." (The revivalist was a controversialist.) "You don't have to believe all that he preaches," replied Dr. Aven. "Believe the Bible. Being a Christian is not just assenting to certain doctrines but coming into a living, personal relationship with Jesus Christ as Savior and Lord" (Virginia Howell Tape, July 7, 1977). This was the major premise.

To Gaines the conclusion was a life-changing experience. Accustomed to regard Christians as church members whose major concern was with doctrine, he found it difficult to accept the view that doctrine and belief in Christ are not the same. Doctrine is important, but first come the claims of Christ. "Test these claims," challenged Dr. Aven. For Gaines, a rationalist, this was difficult to do. Was not mankind responsible for the discovery of electricity, the telephone, the gasoline engine, the "miracles" of the twentieth century? Yes, for God uses humans as instruments, but (major premise) knowledge exists beyond the range of man's intellect. Access to this knowledge (minor premise) requires acceptance by faith of belief in Christ. As Gaines wrote in an early devotional talk (1908?):

> The glory of Christianity is that it does not force the will. Men must choose for themselves [conclusion] in order to reach their highest attainments. Moral sonship cannot be imposed on an evil and sinful nature. Christianity respects personality, individuality (Quoted from Mullins, *Why Is Christianity True?* 1905).

The individual must choose—as Gaines had chosen, recognizing his faults but seeking to overcome them by applying the principles of Christ to himself and to others.

On October 28, 1906, in the college chapel (the church) Gaines Dobbins publicly confessed his belief in Christ as his Savior. As he came forward the evangelist placed his hand on Gaines' shoulder and said, "I seem to feel that someday you will be a Christian minister" *(The Sunday School Builder,* Oct. 1966). But Gaines had no intention of becoming a minister. He sought to follow God's will as a journalist, a reporter, or editor of a city paper, not as a jasper (a Holy Joe).

The direction of Gaines' life had changed, not his vocation. Yet there was a considerable difference between the Gaines Dobbins of October 1906, and his counterpart of October 1905. In 1905, although he was highly respected by his instructors, he was disliked by some of his classmates, particularly the ministerial students, whom he ridiculed and shocked. He was, as he later acknowledged, too studious, too intense, too aloof to make friends indiscriminately with those his own age. Wordsworth-like, rather than participate in college activities, he preferred to walk alone over the hills and gullies of Clinton, stopping under a tree now and then to write down his thoughts. Then, on October 28, something happened.

"In the service that morning," he wrote, simply, "a strange peace came. My doubts faded. . . . Life now took a different turn" *(Great Teachers Make a Difference).* In a sense Gaines' enrollment at Mississippi College should be dated October 28, 1906, instead of a year earlier, for in October 1906, shedding his aloofness, he began to attend church regularly. At first Dr. Lipsey's sermons seemed dry; then Gaines began to listen. Point of view frequently makes a difference. He began to realize that Dr. Lipsey's sermons actually were not boring but stimulating, well reasoned, the type of discourse which Gaines, an intellectual, understood and enjoyed. Having "joined" the church, in that he began to engage in extracurricular activities, Gaines also "joined" the college. In 1906 he was elected editor of *L'Allegro,* the first Mississippi College annual. In 1907 he became editor of the college newspaper, *The Mississippi Collegian* (no copies of which apparently exist), Philomathean editor (coeditor) of *The Mississippi College Magazine,* and manager of the baseball team. Each of these activities took him away from his studies. (Incidentally, in 1908 Mississippi College won 11, tied 2, and lost 7 games, a creditable record.) Yet his grades did not suffer. Instead they improved. In 1905-1906 he earned a 2.4 average (on a 3.0 scale); in 1906-1907, a 2.7 average; in 1907-1908, a 3.0 average to graduate as valedictorian or First Honor Man of his class.

The point of the statistics is not that extracurricular activities are preferable to curricular but that in his Senior year, as a result of his conversion experience, Gaines was confronted with the conflicting claims of two differing types of education. According to the "transmissive" theory, the traditional theory of education, education is primarily concerned with content. According to the "person-centered" or "creative" theory, the primary concern of education is its effect upon individuals. To Professor Patterson and Dr. Aven, education was primarily person-centered (Christ-centered). Gaines agreed. (No one who has studied under Dr. Dobbins, however, would say that he regarded content as unimportant.) Education may be transmissive. Christian education requires knowledge of facts and concern for human personality as well. Which is of greater value? In 1907 Gaines began to recognize that education is at its best when it combines content with involvement, commitment to and participation in the claims of Christ. The view later was supported by his study of Dewey, Kilpatrick, Coe, and others. In 1907 his discovery was based upon personal experience

No longer simply a spectator, in his Senior year (1907-1908) Gaines became one of the most popular students at Mississippi College. He was a Christian. He should have been happy. Yet he still was not satisfied. How could he, a boy who had been brought up in a printing office, expect to amount to anything? Was he not just as much a hypocrite as those whom he had criticized in the past? "Most of my life," he wrote in 1908,

> has been spent in the ink and oil and grime of a printing office among associates many of whom were brutal, vulgar, wicked to the last extreme. I have tried to keep my ideals high, but I have grown up crude, in many ways uncultured, lacking much that goes to make a gentleman (Letter to May Riley, December 4, 1908). . . . Sometimes it seems I *can not* break away from my old plans, my old ambitions. Sometimes I distrust my own self. Sometimes I lose faith in my own honesty and sincerity (Letter to May Riley, February 19, 1909).

How unsuited he was, in his own opinion, to be an instrument of God's will.

What was God's will? Disappointed in himself—a reaction frequently felt by Christians—despite his popularity, Gaines experienced a period of depression. Fortunately (providentially) in October 1907, he became reacquainted with May Virginia Riley, a Senior at Hillman Institute, a school for young ladies also located at Clinton. He had met Miss Riley earlier at a concert, apparently in the spring of 1906. She was not the slightest bit interested in him, nor was he in her. She had a beau, and he was more interested in books than in young ladies. In 1907 the situation was different. As editor of the newspaper and manager of the baseball team Gaines needed someone to accompany him on social occasions. May Riley, the attractive, vivacious daughter of a prominent Lawrence County (Newhebron) merchant, sister of Franklin L. Riley, the Mississippi historian, and sister-in-law of L. L. Patterson, his high-school teacher, seemed an excellent choice.

Strange. Under ordinary circumstances Gaines and May should never have become reacquainted. In October, Miss Riley should not have been a student at Hillman at all. Instead, six months earlier she should have returned to Newhebron with her college degree. In 1906, however, stricken with an attack of typhoid fever, she had been forced to remain at home during her Senior year. Thus in 1907 she was still a student at Hillman, rather lonely, for her classmates had already graduated. She shouldn't have been a student at Hillman—but she was. Chance? (Surely not!)

In November, Mr. G. S. Dobbins escorted Miss May Riley to "The social event of the month, the reception given by the Senior class of Mississippi College to the Senior and Day pupils of Hillman College" (*Mississippi College Magazine,* December 1907). In February 1908, Miss Riley was escorted to the President's Reception by Jesse L. Boyd.

Gaines' interest began to change. For Miss Riley not only was charming ("the most beautiful girl at Hillman"). She also was "quiet and sweet and unselfish and good and kind-hearted" (Letter to May Riley, January 15, 1909). In April, Gaines escorted May to the reception given the Senior classes by Professor and Mrs. J. L. Johnson. In May they became engaged.

May Riley was a remarkable person. Recognizing Gaines' ability, through love and understanding she restored his confidence in himself. "God bless you for helping me as you do," he wrote to May a week after his letter of February 19, 1909.

> I know that I can rely absolutely on two things: The first is that I shall not fail in whatever I undertake so long as I feel the assurance of God's approval. The second is that your love will hold true and unwavering through everything.

With May at his side, with God's approval of his work, Gaines felt that he could not fail.

Yet he was still uncertain as to what God's purpose was in his life. He could not continue his schooling. Nor could he get married. Mrs. Riley, May's mother, refused even to consider May's marriage before she became twenty-one. Besides, although he had a college degree, he had little money. Indeed, he still owed Mr. Ballard $300. He could work as a printer, a job for which he was qualified. Mr. Martin offered to make Gaines his partner, pay him a percentage of the firm's profits and $100 a month salary. The offer was enticing, but Gaines wanted to be more than a printer. Uncertain of his future, he sought direction through prayer.

His prayers were answered by the offer of a position as instructor of English and German at South Mississippi College (now William Carey College), Hattiesburg, an offer that frankly was not very appealing. South Mississippi College, a school which consisted of two frame buildings, was small and poorly endowed. He would be expected to teach 5 classes—4 sections of English, 1 of German. His salary would be considerably less than the $100 a month Mr. Martin offered. Yet his professors recommended that he accept the position. "The experience will be invaluable," Dr. Aven insisted. "Teaching will enable you to organize your thoughts, to respond under pressure, and to face situations that require maturity and tact." Almost passively, following the advice of his professors, in September 1908, Gaines became an instructor at South Mississippi College. He was a good teacher. He worked hard at his classes. He sponsored athletics (baseball). He "took his pastor's place" (preached) occasionally when A. L. O'Briant, his pastor, was absent, taught Sunday School and furnished leadership for the BYPU at Immanuel Baptist Church, then located across the street from the campus.

Yet he still lacked purpose, a difficulty of which Gaines was keenly aware. In May 1909, delivering the baccalaureate address at South Mississippi College, he spoke on the subject, "The Man with a Purpose." "Today," he said,

> is the age of the man with a mission, of the man who says, "This one thing I do." The widening of man's horizons, the complexity of society, and the marvelous advance in science and philosophy have combined to force the individual of the present to be a specialist, if he would not sink into the oblivion of mediocrity, or perish in the wreck of the unfit *(The Progress,* May 22, 1909).

These were inspiring words, words suitable for Commencement. Gaines was determined to avoid mediocrity. He desired to fulfill God's will, but he was uncertain what this will was. Fulfilling God's will requires that man's will be surrendered first. In 1908-1909 Gaines had not surrendered himself fully. Thus he drifted, apparently going nowhere, actually becoming refined by experience to fulfill God's purpose.

Again and again the compulsion of God's will appears in the life of Gaines Dobbins. He had no intention of going to Mississippi College. He went to Mississippi College. He had no intention of going to Southern Seminary. He went to Southern. What led Gaines Dobbins to attend Southern Baptist Theological Seminary, the school at which, beginning in 1920, he taught for more than thirty-six years? To this question his answer was the same that he gave concerning his public confession of faith on October 28, 1906. "When the invitation came, my feet just walked me down the aisle. I was compelled to do it."

Similarly, in 1909, although at the time he would have scoffed at the idea that his decision would lead him to become a minister, his feet (as it were) took over. Step by step, uncertain of the pathway, yet willingly he followed in the direction of his Master. Direction came in the form of licensing, without his knowledge or permission, by the congregation of Immanuel Baptist, Gaines' church. This highly unusual action Gaines accepted as a sign of God's will. The pastor, a graduate of Southern, urged Gaines to attend the Seminary. Then, while on a recruiting trip to Hattiesburg, Dr. George B. Eager, professor of homiletics at Southern, visited South Mississippi College to suggest to Gaines, perceptively, that Christian vocations require Christian training. Gaines' formal study of the Bible consisted of two courses in Old and New Testament, which he had taken at Mississippi College during his Sophomore and Junior years. If he were sincere in his desire to become a Christian journalist, Dr. Eager maintained, Gaines would profit more from taking courses in Bible at Southern than he would in taking courses in journalism at a university. He could take his graduate training later. (Besides, at Southern there was no charge for tuition. According to the catalog, expenses for eight months were less than $170.)

In September 1909, resolved to become a *Christian* journalist, Gaines matriculated at Southern Seminary. Since Southern did not grant degrees to unordained students, he knew that he could not obtain a degree. The regulation did not bother him, however, since he expected to attend Southern only for a year, then go on to Columbia or some other school for training in journalism. More important was the type of instruction which the Seminary offered. The Seminary's buildings, of course, were inadequate. The phrase "of course" is used deliberately, for during this period few Southern Baptist schools had adequate facilities. In 1909, although built within the past 12 to 22 years, the Seminary's four buildings, Norton Hall, the classroom building, New York Hall, the dormitory, Memorial Library (with 20,000 volumes), and Levering Gymnasium, already were too small to provide for Southern's enrollment. As Gaines had learned at Mississippi College, however, "Buildings do not a college make."

In 1909 Southern Seminary was composed both of a remarkable student body and faculty. Of 303 students, only 49 resided in Kentucky. Sixteen came from foreign countries (China, Sweden, England, Australia, Canada, Mexico, Canal Zone, and Brazil), 238 from 26 different states. Included in the group were graduates from 125 different colleges. By comparison, with its preponderance of students from Mississippi, Mississippi College was provincial. Even more unusual was Southern's faculty: John R. Sampey, A. T. Robertson, William J. McGlothlin (Gaines' major professor), W. O. Carver, E. Y. Mullins,

George B. Eager, Byron DeMent, and Charles S. Gardner—giants among men.

Like the prophets of old, each triggers images: Dr. Sampey, fingers drumming on the table, versatile, evangelistic; Dr. Robertson, awesome in his scholarship, demanding, yet humble; Dr. McGlothlin, factural and historical; Dr. Carver, missions-inspired and original; Dr. Mullins, penetrating, insightful; Dr. Gardner, soul-hungry and controversial. To Gaines, who had become accustomed to the teaching methods of Dr. Aven and Professor Patterson, the techniques employed by most of his professors were old-fashioned. (Great educators are not always great teachers.) At the Seminary, classroom procedure was largely a matter of listening to lectures and responding with recitations based on memorization of textual assignments. Recitations under, say, Dr. Robertson, Gaines discovered, could be painful, but, he also discovered, listening to lectures need not be frustrating when the lecturer was as masterful as Dr. Mullins. He preferred the discussion techniques used by Dr. Carver; yet he soon learned that, despite their emphasis on content, his professors were sincerely Christ-centered in their teaching and earnest in presenting the claims of Christ.

Moreover, he discovered, the professors at Southern were more than teachers (preachers, administrators). They were widely respected authors as well. Dr. Eager had been right in suggesting that he should attend the Seminary. Southern, to be sure, was a school of theology, not a school of journalism. However, at Southern the principles of journalism were well understood. Dr. Carver wrote a weekly column for the *Baptist World.* Dr. Mullins was editor of the recently established Seminary journal, *The Baptist Review and Expositor* (1904). Dr. Robertson averaged publishing a book a year. In 50 years, from 1859, the year of the Seminary's founding, to 1909, the eighteen professors at Southern published 60 books (including syllabi), 37 of which had been published from 1899 to 1909 by the eight professors currently on the staff.

Gaines' introduction to the leaders of both the Southern and Northern (American) Baptist Conventions was the direct result of the Seminary's interest in journalism On September 28, the morning after he arrived in Louisville, Gaines received a call from Dr. J. N. Prestridge, editor of the *Baptist World* (competitor of the *Western Recorder).* The call was not just a matter of chance. Gaines had written Dr. Mullins, the president of the Seminary, of his qualifications as a printer and of his need to work. The letter interested Dr. Mullins, for not only was Dr. Mullins a Mississippian but as a young boy he also had been a printer. Dr. Mullins recommended Gaines to Dr. Prestridge. Dr. Lowery, the president of Mississippi College, also had written Dr. Prestridge, suggesting that he employ Gaines as a printer. To Gaines, the possibility of working for the *Baptist World* was almost a miracle. Dr. Prestridge offered him a job as a printer at 35 cents an hour ($20 to $25 a month, more than enough to pay expenses!) *and* proposed that, since he was a competent reporter, Gaines cover the events of the Seminary's Jubilee Celebration scheduled to begin on September 29. On Dr. Prestridge's recommendation, Dr. Mullins unhesitatingly introduced Gaines, an unknown, to Dr. Henry Newman (Waco), Dr. Shailer Mathews (Chicago), Dr. Joseph Gilmour (Toronto), and other notables of the Celebration. Although he no longer was a journalist, Dr. Mullins recognized the value of publicity. With his approval, writing for the *Baptist World*, from October 1909, to June 1910, Gaines wrote 23 (signed) articles and publicity releases for the Seminary. (Ten years later, in part because he was aware of Dr. Dobbins' ability as a journalist, Dr. Mullins asked Dr. Dobbins to return to Southern to establish the Department of Church Efficiency and Sunday School Pedagogy.)

Initially Gaines expected to remain at Southern only a year. As he became acquainted with his professors, however, his attitude began to change.

> E. Y. Mullins was reconciling theology with science and psychology; W. O. Carver was teaching a course in "Christianity and Current Thought"; John R. Sampey and A. T. Robertson were interpreting Old and New Testaments in the light of historical research; W. J. McGlothlin was teaching church history according to the facts and not Landmark presuppositions; Charles S. Gardner was pioneering in the application of the Christian gospel and ethic to social issues *(The Baptist Program*, Oct. 1968).

These were men who not only knew the Bible but also recognized the need for its presentation in contemporary terms. Their teaching methods might be outmoded but their subject matter was anything but stereotyped. Apparently a year was too short a time to plumb the depths of the Bible! In her letters May shared Gaines' excitement. According to the Seminary catalog, two could live almost as cheaply as one. (Living expenses for a married couple supposedly required only $10 more a month.) Thus in December 1909, during the Seminary's customary two-day Christmas recess, Gaines returned to Mississippi to marry his college sweetheart, May Riley, on Christmas Eve. Neither was particularly concerned about finances, for he could always earn a living as a printer.

May Riley was a wonderful helpmeet. Regardless of what the future might hold, she committed herself and her husband to God. The daughter of moderately wealthy parents, nevertheless she happily accepted the privations of student life. Although she was not always in good health, she ably seconded Gaines in his (their) church work, using her degree in music in playing the piano or the pump organ, teaching Sunday School, working with the Woman's Missionary Union, attending Seminary lectures in Old and New Testament with her husband (attending classes which, before 1903, women ordinarily were not permitted to attend).

As students, from 1910 to 1912 the newly married couple lived lives that were relatively uneventful with three exceptions. Their $50 a month income (classes until 4; work at the print shop from four to seven in the evenings, all day Monday and Saturday) had to be guarded carefully, but God blessed them and life was good. From June through November 1910, Gaines and May remained in Hattiesburg where, on September 22, Gaines Stanley Dobbins, Jr., was born. Missing the fall quarter at the Seminary was necessary so that Gaines might work an extra three months to pay for the baby. (Regardless of what the Seminary catalog indicated, living expenses for a family of three required more than $40 a month!) In 1911 Gaines and May faced serious financial problems, so much so that from May 1911, to September 1912, they remained in Hattiesburg, where Gaines again worked as a printer. In January 1912, Gaines undertook his first regular preaching assignment, at New Augusta, a small town 15 miles from Hattiesburg. He was not ordained, but Baptist polity permitted "licensed ministers" to preach. "The church was small and struggling, the people were few and scattered," he recalled,

> but they loved me for what I was trying to do and asked me to undertake the task. I had no revival sermons. However, we had been studying the Book of Romans at the Seminary and I decided just to preach on the high spots of this

great book (Letter to Kenneth Stringer, Pastor, First Baptist Church, New Augusta, March 23, 1965).

During the August revival, 24 came forward for membership, 11 for baptism, 7 by letter, 6 by statement. Later, at the river baptismal service, the young minister's (borrowed) baptismal suit developed a leak. As a result he had a firm foundation; had he fallen, however, he would have drowned. It took six deacons to carry him back to the shore.

On August 25, Gaines resigned his position as pastor of New Augusta. Two weeks later, on September 9, 1912, he made a momentous decision. With May's full approval he withdrew from the printer's union. (The certificate indicating "Honorable Withdrawal" he kept in his lockbox until he died.) No longer would—or could—he work as a printer. Instead, before returning to the Seminary, Gaines surrendered himself fully to God. On June 18, 1913, at Walnut Street Baptist Church, Lousiville, Gaines Dobbins was "publicly ordained to the work of the Gospel Ministry." Three weeks earlier, on May 27, he received his Th.M.

On July 27, 1913, according to the *Western Recorder,* the new minister became pastor of the Thirty-Sixth and Grand Baptist Church ("Louisville Mission," later Baptist Temple at Thirty-Sixth and Kentucky). Actually he had begun working at the church nine months earlier as an assignment in Dr. Carver's course in missions. As a beginning pastor Gaines was unusually successful. When he began his pastorate officially, apparently on June 22, the church had 60 members and an average Sunday School attendance of 58. A year later, after a tent revival in which "41 were added to the church, 25 for baptism, 16 by letter and under watchcare," the membership of the church had increased to 120, with a Sunday School attendance of 152. Since the church could not afford a visiting evangelist, as the pastor, Gaines conducted the revival himself.

To Gaines, preaching at Temple was a rewarding experience. For his sermon topics at New Augusta he had used "borrowed" material. At Temple his topics were of his own selection. (Of his 40 sermons reported by the *Baptist World* and the *Western Recorder,* 26 were based on texts from Matthew, John, Luke, and Acts. One was based on a text from Romans.) One step remained for Gaines to become a minister of the gospel. At Temple, he said, he experienced the *kerygma*. I discovered it myself, and I made my commitment to be a minister of the Gospel of Jesus Christ (Biography I, *c.*1950).

Although he had conducted a successful revival in 1912, it was not until he led the revival at Temple (August 31—September 14, 1913) that he truly felt the power of the call to preach.

Sept. 14. Our two weeks' meeting closed Sunday night. The pastor's preaching has been greatly blessed. The church has been greatly revived and our prospects are bright.
Nov. 9. Money was raised at the morning service to erect a temporary addition to our building pending the building of our new home, which we expect to begin soon.
Dec. 14. A great Sunday. The addition to our building was opened and overcrowded at both services.
Jan. 4. Building movement launched with greatly encouraging prospects ("Pastor's Conference," *Western Recorder).*

For almost two years he had worked in the vineyard, tending it carefully, helping it to grow. Labor in the vineyard (study, preparation), however, was not enough. It was God, through the leadership of the Holy Spirit, who brought about the harvest. Dr. Aven and Professor Patterson had been right. Christ's claims can be tested: "The condition is simple—the casting aside of the old heart, defiled with its selfishness and sin, now broken by repentance, and a turning to him in love and trust" (Trial Sermon, written for Dr. Gardner's class in homiletics, 1912-13). At Temple, Gaines discovered that the dilemma which he had faced in high school—the world's dilemma—can be solved by accepting, committing oneself to, and acting upon the claims of Christ.

3
Minister, Editor

In May 1914, Pastor Dobbins resigned his position at Baptist Temple, Louisville, to accept a call from Galilee Baptist Church, Gloster, Mississippi. In June he received his degree, Th.D., *Magna cum laude*, from Southern Seminary. (Not surprisingly, his doctoral thesis was titled "A History of Southern Baptist Journalism," a study which still has considerable value.) To Dr. Dobbins, as he now had the right to be called, Galilee Church seemed an excellent choice for the beginning of his pastoral ministry. The only full-time church in its association, with over 200 members, "Old Galilee" (1824) was one of the most influential churches in South Mississippi. Moreover, it was located near Hattiesburg and Newhebron, Gaines' and May's homes. Unfortunately, in inviting Dr. Dobbins to become their pastor, the deacons at Galilee had neglected to inform him of one difficulty. Galilee was a split church.

A former minister, Dr. Dobbins was told, had been a staunch Calvinist. From the pulpit he had pointed a loaded pistol at the congregation, declaring, "If I should take this pistol and kill every one of you, it wouldn't have the slightest effect on my salvation" (Howell Tape, 1977). When the congregation objected to this version of "once saved, always saved," the minister (M. T. Martin) organized another church, the Gloster (Liberty Street) Baptist Church, which met a few blocks away. The split had occurred 18 years earlier. By 1914 the cause of the controversy had largely been forgotten, but members of the two congregations were still unfriendly.

As pastor of Galilee, Dr. Dobbins tried to bridge the gap—he was warned to have nothing to do with the members of the other church. Galilee had an active Woman's Missionary Union. Otherwise the church seemed uninterested in missions. It contributed generously to a building program designed to provide adequate space for its Sunday School, yet it showed little desire to organize its school efficiently and depended for its operating funds upon subscriptions collected irregularly from its members. To his dismay, Dr. Dobbins discovered that sometimes his salary was paid when it was due; sometimes it wasn't. Finances, he was told, were the business of the deacons, not the minister. Yet Galilee had some of the finest Christians he had ever met. What should he do? Apparently the church expected him to be a preacher rather than a pastor. He should have investigated conditions at Galilee before he came, but he hadn't. And he knew virtually nothing about church administration—a subject which had been almost ignored at the Seminary.

Acting for the first time as a "doctor of sick churches" (DSC, a title given him later by Dr. John R. Sampey), Dr. Dobbins proposed a wise but drastic solution to the major problem:

> If he [the other pastor] would resign, I would also, and we would seek to lead the two churches to unite and call the same pastor. Where would I go? I didn't know but I trusted the Lord to provide *(The Alabama Baptist*, Oct. 23, 1969).

It took considerable faith to make a proposal of this nature, for pulpit changes are not always easy to obtain. Moreover, although Brother Johnson, Liberty Street's third pastor, and Dr. Dobbins served opposing congregations, neither really wished to change pastorates. Each preferred to remain where he was. Pastor J. R. Johnson ("a good old man, very gifted") insisted that, since his call came from God, he was predestined to remain at Liberty Street. To Dr. Dobbins the situation was frustrating. Not only was Galilee his first real pastorate but he believed that "practically without exception the most successful churches are those that have long pastorates." The quotation is from *Building Better Churches* (1947). However, it presents an idea which Dr. Dobbins expressed frequently in his writings *(Western Recorder*, March 27, 1930; *The Sunday School Builder*, March 1955; *The Alabama Baptist*, April 9, 1970). A successful church requires "at least five year's service," yet at Galilee a short pastorate apparently was the only means by which Galilee and Liberty Street could be reconciled. Providentially, in March 1916, the situation was resolved. Both pastors were called to other churches, Dr. Dobbins to the First Baptist Church of New Albany, a bustling commercial center in northeastern Mississippi. Under the leadership of Galilee's new pastor, Jessie L. Boyd, in 1917 Galilee and Liberty Street were reunited.

In his work at Galilee, Dr. Dobbins considered himself largely a failure. Actually the opposite was true. On July 1, 1915, the *Baptist Record* summarized the opinion of his fellow pastors:

> Brother Dobbins is one of the most aggressive and devoted pastors to be found anywhere. . . . By his untiring efforts, Christian walk, and good guidance he has greatly built up [Galilee] Church and perfected its organizations and made possible the erection of a handsome house of worship with seemingly little effort on the part of the congregation. (The editor of the *Baptist Record*, Dr. P. I. Lipsey, was the pastor at Clinton in 1906.)

As pastor of Galilee, Dr. Dobbins began to attract favorable attention. In August 1914, at Gillsburg he held a revival which resulted in the addition to the church of 31 members, 27 by baptism. During the revival, he suffered an attack of appendicitis for which he was hospitalized in September. As a result the revival at Galilee scheduled for September was postponed until November—apparently fortunately. For in November the revival which he conducted at Galilee resulted in the addition of over 40 members, 37 being baptized the last night of the meeting. By December the church had increased 25 percent in membership (53 members), $3,000 to $4,000 had been subscribed for church repairs and improvements, and, an even more significant development, the young people of Gloster began to attend the church in large numbers. Under Dr. Dobbins' leadership the church had begun to revive.

In 1915, Dr. Dobbins began to expand his activities. In January, along with E. Y. Mullins, P. I. Lipsey, J. M. Frost, I. J. Van Ness, and others, he taught in the South Mississippi Bible School at Hattiesburg. In May, seven years after he was graduated from Mississippi College, he returned to Clinton to preach the baccalaureate sermon at Hillman. In June, at Galilee he dedicated the church's new building and preached a revival that added 14 to the church. In November, Dr. Dobbins became a member of the Publications Commission of the Mississippi Baptist Convention. In January 1916, associated with Victor Masters, J. W. Porter, and others, at the South Mississippi Bible School he was asked to repeat the lectures he had given the preceding year on "Homiletics, As Seen in the Preaching of Jesus."

In March 1916, Dr. Dobbins became pastor of First Church, New

Albany. In April, at the Chickasaw Association Meeting in Cornersville, he spoke on the subject of "God's Plan of the Ages." The address, which the *Baptist Record* termed "the greatest missionary sermon that had ever been preached at Cornersville," was noted widely, for in 1916 Mississippi Baptists were not strongly missionary. First Church, New Albany, enthusiastically supported its new pastor's point of view. In November the church reported gifts of over $1,300 to State, Home, and Foreign Missions, $50 more than its pastor's salary and approximately one fourth of the church's annual budget.

At Cornersville Dr. Dobbins also spoke on the subject of the Sunday School, as he did whenever he had the opportunity. Wherever he served, whether at Temple, Gillsburg, Galilee, Cornersville—or later, at Eastland (Nashville), New Salem (Cox's Creek), Walnut Street, or Crescent Hill (Louisville), Dr. Dobbins presented the Sunday School as the educational, teacher-training, evangelistic, soul-winning arm of the church. Thus in April, immediately after he had become pastor at New Albany, he began to reorganize the Sunday School of First Church into a graded system and to plan for an adequate Sunday School building. (At New Albany in 1979 the older members of the church remembered Dr. Dobbins as "the Organizer.") As a result, associated with P. E. Burroughs, Kathleen Mallory, and other denominational leaders, in July, at the Blue Mountain Encampment he was asked to demonstrate his concepts of effective Sunday School teaching. In August, Riley Franklin Dobbins, the second member of the "Dobbins' Home Sunday School," was born.

In 1916, Dr. Dobbins was a successful minister. He was a bit overeducated for his position, perhaps, but no matter. He was performing a useful task. Then, apparently in March, Dr. Dobbins took a step that changed his life. Revising the lectures he had given at South Mississippi Bible School, he wrote three lessons for the *Convention Teacher* (September 1916), the teacher-training quarterly of the Baptist Sunday School Board. Earlier, in 1915-16, he had written a series of articles on Baptist periodicals for the *Baptist Record*. In October 1916, his writing led to an invitation from Dr. James M. Frost, the Corresponding Secretary of the Sunday School Board, to join the editorial staff of the Board as founding editor (1916-32) of *Home and Foreign Fields*, the combined journal of the Home and Foreign Mission Boards.

Called to Nashville for an interview, to his dismay he found Dr. Frost on his deathbed.

> He clasped his wan hand in mine and said, "Dobbins, the Board needs you. Van Ness [the Editorial Secretary] can't do the work by himself. Indications are all in favor of your giving that help. You are equipped for it. A great door and effectual will be opened for you."
>
> He was seized with a fit of coughing and the nurse motioned for us to leave. As we left Dr. Van Ness was almost in tears. He said, "That's it. I wouldn't have said that by myself, but he's Secretary of the Board. He thinks it's the Lord's will for you to come and be my helper. I think that settles it" (Biography I, *c.* 1950; *The Alabama Baptist*, Oct. 30, 1969; Badgett Dillard Tape, Aug. 7, 1978).

Dr. Dobbins' was one of fifteen to twenty names recommended to Dr. Van Ness, Dr. Frost's assistant, as possible candidates for the position. "Providentially [Acts 1:26]," Dr. Dobbins wrote, "as Dr. Van Ness thumbed through the names, which had been placed on cards, my name was on the top each time he finished with the cards." Dr. Dobbins, who was ordained, trained as a journalist, missionary minded, and relatively well-known by the leaders of the denomination, was the most suitable candidate for the editorship.

The selection placed Dr. Dobbins in a quandary. Riley was less than three months old. Mrs. Dobbins was in no condition to travel. He had a responsibility to New Albany, where he had been pastor only a little more than seven months. He had thought that he was fulfilling God's will in his work as a minister. Yet if it was God's will—as Dr. Frost believed it was—that he return to journalism, if New Albany would release him without prejudice, then he would accept his new position without hesitation. He had no other choice.

On November 1, 1916, Dr. Dobbins became editor of *Home and Foreign Fields*, a 32-40 page continuation of *Home Field* and *Foreign Mission Journal*, periodicals which the Convention, in an economy mood, had ordered discontinued as of October. Immediately he ran into difficulties. Because of the war, printing costs had risen. By the end of the first fiscal year (April 30, 1917), with receipts of $9,295, *Home and Foreign Fields* had incurred a deficit of $6,031.45, a loss of approximately $1,000 a month. Six thousand dollars was a considerable sum. In 1917-18 the receipts of the Board itself were little more than half a million dollars. To the business manager, Mr. Archie Dunaway, whose motto was "Throw away, go away," the situation was, to say the least, disturbing. Yet the Convention had instructed the Board to publish the magazine.

The Sunday School Board welcomed the opportunity to serve the cause of missions; it was less willing to publish *Home and Foreign Fields* at financial loss. In 1919-20 the Board raised the subscription price of *Home and Foreign Fields* from 50 cents to 75 cents, then from 75 cents to one dollar. Circulation dropped. Attempting to reverse the trend, Dr. Dobbins wrote to pastors and Woman's Missionary Union leaders throughout the Convention, obtaining the names of members who would act as "agents" for the magazine. With the cooperation of the editors of the State Baptist newspapers, he devised a plan for joint subscriptions (*Baptist Record* and *Home and Foreign Fields*, $2.00 a year). Circulation increased from 25,000 to 67,000. In 1921, due to increasing costs, the joint subscription plan was discontinued. Circulation decreased but leveled out around 36,000.

Throughout its 21 years of publication *Home and Foreign Fields* failed to gain popular support. Why? Three to four million Southern Baptists should have subscribed willingly to a journal which "by means of thrilling articles and stories, profusely illustrated by pictures from the fields . . . sought *to make missions real*" (*The Sunday School Builder*, Dec. 1927). Except for a series of letters (1930-34) between Dr. Dobbins and Dr. J. B. Lawrence, Secretary of the Home Mission Board, few records of Dr. Dobbins' term as editor of *Home and Foreign Fields* exist. Study of the contents of the magazine, however, indicates that, aside from financial difficulties, he faced three problems: (1) The necessity of publishing a missionary magazine without prior commitment from missionaries to contribute articles for the magazine; (2) lack of support among Southern Baptists for organized missionary endeavor; and (3) ineffective planning by the boards and agencies of the Convention.

The enthusiastic response of Cynthia Miller, C. T. Willingham, George Green, Victor Masters, J. F. Love, and other Mission Board contributors suggests that the first problem, referred to in the "Prospectus" of the first (November) issue of *Home and Foreign Fields*, actually was not a problem at all. Obtaining contributors involved work, the writing of numerous letters and attending planning sessions at state conventions, but to Dr. Dobbins, writing and listening was seldom a burden.

Loving Christ, he loved people. As a result he was, as has frequently been noted, one of the friendliest and most approachable of Southern Baptist leaders. The second problem was more difficult to resolve. Why so few subscribers to *Home and Foreign Fields*? To this question, a theological answer is that before World War I a number of Baptists regarded mission boards as unscriptural. According to the Landmark view, only the local church has authority to send out missionaries. It was not until *after* 1909, with the publication of Dr. W. O. Carver's *Missions in the Plan of the Ages*, observed Dr. Dobbins (in *Baptist History and Heritage*, October 1979), that Southern Baptists as a group accepted the concept of organized missions as being scriptural. In 1917 not all Southern Baptists regarded organized missions as a biblical means of implementing the Great Commission. Circulation of *Home and Foreign Fields* suffered as a result.

As editor of *Home and Foreign Fields* Dr. Dobbins faced a third, interrelated but more practical, difficulty. In 1917 as a denomination the Convention was ineffectively organized. (The Cooperative Program was not instituted until 1925.) Throughout the Convention, Sunday after Sunday offerings were taken for worthy causes: the orphanage, the hospital, the building fund, ministerial relief, education, home missions, foreign missions, state missions, and so forth. In 1917 Southern Baptists observed four mission days. Twice a year the Sunday School sponsored "Missionary Day in the Sunday School," at Christmas for foreign missions and at Easter for home missions. The Woman's Missionary Union also sponsored two Missionary Days, the "Lottie Moon Offering" at Christmas (the Christmas Offering) for foreign missions and the "Annie Armstrong (Self-Denial, Thank) Offering" at Easter for home missions. The Woman's Missionary Union vigorously supported the Sunday School offerings—indeed, not only was "Missionary Day in the Sunday School" originally a WMU project but nine tenths of *Home and Foreign Fields'* readers were members of the Union. Nevertheless the two sets of offerings competed with each other, resulting in inadequate funds being raised by both groups. Seeking to avoid duplication of effort, as the Sunday School Board's "Mission Specialist," as early as 1928 Dr. Dobbins suggested that the Lottie Moon and Annie Armstrong Offerings become a joint WMU and Convention-wide project. Dr. Van Ness approved the suggestion. However, fearing that the offerings might be diverted from mission causes, the WMU objected to the proposal. It was not until 1960 that Sunday School Board efforts toward raising mission offerings were given up in favor of the WMU offerings.

From 1916-32, as editor of *Home and Foreign Fields*, Dr. Dobbins faced a difficult task. The circulation of the magazine could be increased, but only at considererable cost. Cost, however, was not the major problem. The basic purpose of a missions' magazine is communication. Communication requires shared assumptions. During the period in which Dr. Dobbins was editor of *Home and Foreign Fields*, obviously the Boards and Southern Baptists did not share these assumptions. Thus the major function of *Home and Foreign Fields*, as Dr. Dobbins conceived it, was to "indoctrinate" (educate) pastors, deacons, superintendents, teachers, the leaders of the local churches, in the significance of the missionary cause. What were the duties of the Home and Foreign Boards? Who were the missionaries? What were their problems, their successes and failures? And more important, to what extent is the cause of Christ the cause of missions? In articles written by the missionaries, *Home and Foreign Fields* sought to present the who, what, how, and where of missions. In his editorials Dr. Dobbins sought to explain the why of missions.

For sixteen years, in 491 editorials in *Home and Foreign Fields*, and for 62 years, in more than 170 articles (programs, lessons, editorials) in other Sunday School periodicals, Dr. Dobbins presented missions as the central and unifying aim of the church. Of what value, he asked, are Sunday School classes, worship services, the WMU, Brotherhood, or any other agency of the church unless their purpose is to spread the gospel?

> Home Missions, Foreign Missions, State Missions, Sunday Schools, B.Y.P.U., W.M.U., Men's Brotherhood, Benevolences, Christian Education, all have the same fundamental missionary purpose, and are bound together in the same bundle of missionary ends. They rise or fall, succeed or fail, together. Constructively and unfailingly *Home and Foreign Fields* has stood for and stood by the principle of cooperation (*The Sunday School Builder*, Dec. 1927).

As editor of *Home and Foreign Fields* Dr. Dobbins avoided direct controversy. Nevertheless, if there is a single theme that runs through the journal, it is that of the necessity for Baptists to remain true to the model of the New Testament church. To Dr. Dobbins, as to Dr. Carver, the

New Testament church was a cooperative and cooperating body of believers who, to increase their fruitfulness, voluntarily associated themselves into larger groups. In other words, organization in itself is not unscriptural so long as it remains under the control of the local church. This is the teaching of Romans 15:26, 1 Corinthians 16:1, as well as other passages in the Bible. Thus organized missions (missions "well" or "worthily supported," 3 John 5-6) is a biblical means of spreading the gospel.

How successful was Dr. Dobbins as editor of *Home and Foreign Fields*? The question is difficult to answer, for "success" is a word which is difficult to define. In terms of circulation, although in number of subscriptions it increased 44 percent, *Home and Foreign Fields* was not a success. In terms of providing the basis for future harvest, however, the magazine was an unqualified success. Though not a missions board, as Dr. P. E. Burroughs suggested (in *Fifty Fruitful Years*, 1941), from its beginning the Sunday School Board "sought to be what every Christian institution must be, missionary, intensely missionary." *Home and Foreign Fields* provided three of the Convention's major agencies, the Sunday School Board, the Home Mission Board, and the Foreign Mission Board, a means by which each could implement missions cooperatively, the principal business of the Convention. Willingly supporting the new venture, in September 1918, the Sunday School Board added to Dr. Dobbins' duties the responsibility of conducting a weekly missionary column in *The Organized Class Magazine*, the Sunday School journal. In January 1919, Dr. Dobbins became editor of a second missionary column in *Kind Words,* the Board's oldest publication. In June 1919, reshaping its organization, the Board instituted a new administrative department, the Department of Missionary Publications, with Dr. Dobbins as head.

To Southern Baptists, during the period of his editorship, Dr. Dobbins ("Mr. Missions") wrote with the authority of the Board. During the first year of *Home and Foreign Fields'* publication, this statement was literally true. On October 31, 1916, Dr. Frost, the Corresponding Secretary of the Board, died. Dr. Van Ness, the Editorial Secretary, became Corresponding Secretary (Executive Secretary). Thus, during the winter of 1916-17, Dr. Dobbins was the only full-time Sunday School editor at the Sunday School Board. (Dr. Landrum Leavell edited the BYPU publications.) "On 'Big Thursday,' the Thursday before the new quarter began," Dr. Dobbins recalled,

> all of us went down to the mailing room, put on our aprons, and I joined the group, mailing literature which was carried to the post office in a pickup truck. I would wrap and tie and somebody else would paste on the labels. . . . When I joined the Board there were only three people on the editorial staff, Dr. Van Ness, who continued to be the chief editor, myself, and a Presbyterian lady, Miss Marian Phelps, who edited *Kind Words*, prepared copy for the printer, and read proof. Mrs. Forbes and Mrs. Van Ness did some writing. Miss Annie Williams and Arthur Flake were in charge of the field work. We can never be too thankful for Arthur Flake. He laid foundations that we ought never to forsake (*Quarterly Review*, April 1968; "Sunday School Improvement in the Immediate Future," Speech, Sunday School Board, Oct. 2, 1973; Dillard Tape, 1978).

Upon Dr. Dobbins' shoulders fell the responsibility of writing and/or editing most of the Board's publications, *Home and Foreign Fields, The Organized Class Magazine, The Home Department Magazine*, quarterlies for Adults, Intermediates, and Juniors, leaflets and picture lesson cards for children. (The quarterlies were priced at two to four cents, leaflets at one cent, picture lesson cards at two-and-a-half cents.) As "Senior Editor," technically Dr. Dobbins was the superior of Dr. E. C. Dargan and Dr. Hight C Moore, who joined the editorial staff in 1917. Particularly with regard to Dr. Dargan, former professor at Southern Seminary and president of the Convention, Dr. Dobbins remarked, it was a supervision he declined to exercise.

What led the Sunday School Board to entrust Dr. Dobbins, a young man only thirty to thirty-one years of age, with such tremendous responsibility? In part his position as "spokesman" for the Board was due to his relatively errorless writing. As a journalist, Dr. Dobbins was technically trained; moreover, he was a careful student of the Bible. To his regret, occasionally he made mistakes. For example, he recalled, in one lesson he wrote "of Lydia's husband, on the assumption that if she had a 'household' [Acts 16:15] she must have been married—an unwarranted assumption" (*The Alabama Baptist*, Oct. 30, 1969). Errors of interpretations, however, appeared infrequently in his writings. A study of the carbons of some 10,000 letters in the "Dobbins Collections" at Southern Seminary and the Sunday School Board reveals fewer than ten letters of protest concerning his interpretations of Scriptures. The lack of criticism is amazing, for Baptists have never been averse to denouncing views which they regard as unbiblical. Dr. Dobbins—at least to Southern Baptists—was a careful, conscientious student of Scripture. Moreover, his standards for writing man-made literature concerning Scripture basically were those of the Sunday School Board. He was not a "yes man" who defended the Board as being right regardless of its position. Rather he accepted the standards of the Board because its standards were his standards.

What were these standards? The question is worth examining since for 62 years, in the *Baptist Adult Union Quarterly, Sunday School Young People and Adults, Convention Teacher(s), Intermediate Quarterly, Sunday School Builder, Intermediate Graded Lesson Series, Baptist Young People's Magazine, Baptist Adults, Training Union Quarterly for the Deaf, Training Union Simplified, La Fe Bautista*, and other Sunday School periodicals, Dr. Dobbins wrote some 2,571 pupil/teacher lessons or almost 50 years of biblical interpretations. To this figure should be added 903 reviews and articles written for the *Review and Expositor*, 492 educational or pedagogical articles written for Sunday School publications, the most prominent being the *Sunday School Builder, Sunday School Young People and Adults, Convention Teacher(s), Baptist Training Union Magazine*, and *Church Administration*, and 275 articles on religious subjects written for the denominational press, *The Alabama Baptist, Western Recorder,* and *California Southern Baptist* being the most frequent publishers. A prolific writer, from 1916 to 1978 Dr. Dobbins wrote more than 4,900 articles (duplications not counted) and 33 books, 6 of which were translated into foreign languages. Articles written before 1916 are not included. For 62 years, excluding Sundays, he published an average of 400 words a day—some 25,000 pages. At least two of his books, *Deepening the Spiritual Life* (1937) and *The Improvement of Teaching in the Sunday School* (1943; rewritten, 1973), had a circulation of over 100,000 copies. In 1946, the *Baptist Adult Union Quarterly*, a periodical which he founded and for which he wrote for 17 years, had a circulation of nearly 1,000,000 copies.

As a writer Dr. Dobbins is said to have published more Sunday School lesson expositions, more Training Union programs, and more articles dealing with religious education than any other Southern Baptist. What were the standards upon which he based his amazing contribution to Southern Baptist life? (The statements that follow are summarized from his Th.D. thesis, classroom notes, and articles in which he discussed the subject of writing. Particularly valuable is an article titled "Baptist Progress and the Printed Page," which appeared in *The Alabama Baptist*, April 30, 1970. Unnoted quotations are from this article.) To Dr. Dobbins, writing for Christian publications required (requires) adherence to five principles.

1. Commitment by the writer (or editor) to the Bible as "the power of God unto salvation to everyone that believeth" (Romans 1:16). The Bible is the inspired word of God, "the true center of Christian union, and the supreme standard by which all human conduct, creeds, and religious opinions should be tried" (*Philadelphia Confession of Faith*, 1742; *Baptist Faith and Message*, 1925, 1963).
2. Acceptance by the writer of the world-wide mission of Christianity. The purpose of Christian publications is to win others to Christ, at home and abroad; hence evangelization and missions are the inescapable obligation and privilege of every Christian writer.
3. Recognition by the writer that he is a servant of the churches and the denomination. He is not a free-lance, majoring on criticism and controversy, but a journalist who is subject to the same ethical requirements as other responsible denominational servants.
4. Understanding by the writer of his responsibility for molding opinion. "The editor's question, like that of the preacher and teacher, should be: What difference does it make?" Writing that lacks relevance has no place in Christian publications.
5. Ability on the part of the writer to produce copy that is readable: clearly expressed, well-outlined, person-centered. "Some tests of readibility are: attractive make-up, attention-getting headlines, familiar language, short words and sentences, relatively brief articles, variety, and originality."

These five principles largely summarize the contents of the course titled "The Ministry of Writing" which Dr. Dobbins inaugurated and taught at Southern and Golden Gate Seminaries from 1949 to 1966.

In 1917, evaluated on the basis of these principles, in categories 1 through 3 Sunday School Board periodicals would have rated "Superior." So far as categories 4 and 5 are concerned, the Board's publications would have been rated "Deficient." Writers for Christian publications, Dr. Dobbins believed, should lead their readers to relate the teachings of the Bible to life-changing experiences. Instead, in 1917 Sunday School publications tended to be content centered, overly theological, and lacking in reader appeal (criticisms which, somewhat embarrassingly, in 1929 were applied to Dr. Dobbins' lessons in the *Intermediate Lesson Series*). In the *Teacher*, leaders of adults and young people studied the same lesson. Teacher training methods were largely restricted to columns inculcating the "Doctrines of the Lesson." Packaging of the literature was unattractive. Printed on newspaper stock, with narrow margins and "covers that looked like wrapping paper from the meat market" (*Quarterly Review*, April 1968), the quarterlies issued by the Board in the '20s were frankly unappealing.

To Dr. Dobbins, a "repackaging" of Sunday School publications, if the term may be used in its wider meaning, was necessary if the literature of the Board was to become truly effective. Repackaging involves rearrangement of layouts; more basically it involves the use of motivational techniques. Which causes life-changing experiences, transmissive writing, writing which emphasizes content, or person-centered writing, writing which emphasizes reaction and response? To Dr. Dobbins, the Bible itself provided the answer:

> The truth that Jesus taught can never be separated from him, and all efforts to consider his teachings apart from his person have proved unavailing. In like manner the preaching of Paul—or, indeed, of any other man—cannot be fully understood and appreciated apart from his life and labors. The apostle doubted the expediency of the narration of personal matters. . . . We count these words among the most precious from his inspired pen. Their revelation of the man is of inestimable value to us for the understanding and appreciation of his message (*Convention Teacher*, Sept. 1916).

Fifty-six years later Dr. Dobbins, writing more skillfully but with unchanged opinion, considered the same issue:

> What are the ingredients that sustain audience attention in a play, all the way from Sophocles and Shakespeare to the latest TV opera? The ingredients are remarkably simple and similar: a human-interest situation, a problem that creates mounting tension, conflict between the "good guy" and the "bad guy," complications that make the outcome apparently uncertain, struggle that reaches its climax, conclusion—whether happy or unhappy—that brings the action to an appropriate ending. Much of the Bible narrative follows this pattern. . . .

> Take the Exodus saga. The scene is set in ancient Egypt. The characters are God, Jacob, and his family transported from Canaan, the heroic figure of Joseph risen to royal power, the multiplying of Joseph's family to become an enslaved multitude, the checkered career of Moses, the central character, the struggle for emancipation as Moses under divine guidance overpowers the mighty Pharaoh, the flight to the Land of Promise, the eventual settlement in Canaan and fulfillment of the divine purpose. Here is an human-interest drama that sets the blood coursing, surpassing Homer's *Odyssey* or Virgil's *Aeneid* or Shakespeare's *Lear*. . . .
>
> The New Testament Gospels provide material for "the greatest story ever told." The promised Messiah comes at last, in ways foretold but not expected. For thirty years he lives in obscurity, then launches out on the most revolutionary mission ever conceived—the turning of the tide of history, the transformation of humanity, the conquest of sin and death, the shifting of the human condition from emptiness and poverty to fullness and abundance, the infusion of hope where once there was hopelessness. . . .
>
> What a pity when this element is lost and the Bible's preaching and teaching become abstract, uninteresting, didactic, its living, pulsing truths exhibited as historical relics of interest only as reminders of the past! (*The Alabama Baptist*, Feb. 24, 1972).

It was writing that is dramatic, filled with human interest, in a word, person-centered, alive, that Dr. Dobbins coveted for Sunday School Board publications. Apparently he succeeded in his purpose. In 1941 Dr. Louie D. Newton headed a group of consultants who studied the Sunday School literature published by various Protestant denominations. His report is worth quoting:

> In the important matter of technique, including covers, general make-up, and typography, Southern Baptist literature was voted the first place. In the matter of material, by which we mean the wide field of content in lesson treatment, exposition, illustrative articles, doctrinal and devotional articles, our literature was voted first place. In the matter of appeal, from *The Teacher* to the Cradle Roll pictures, our literature was voted first place.

Between 1917 and 1941 a considerable change took place in the quarterlies and journals published by the Sunday School Board. For this change Dr. Dobbins was largely responsible—largely, but by no means completely. The "repackaging" of Sunday School literature began in 1916 with the inauguration of Dr. Isaac J. Van Ness as Secretary of the Board. "His genius," wrote Dr. Dobbins, "lay in his ability to gather about him dedicated men and women who could do the job" (*Great*

Teachers Make a Difference, 1965). To Prince E. Burroughs, Edwin C. Dargan, Arthur Flake, Landrum Leavell, John L. Hill, Hight C Moore, E. E. Lee, William P. Phillips, B. W. Spilman, Harry Strickland, W. S. Wiley, Lilian Forbes, Annie Williams, and a host of others, including Gaines Dobbins, belongs the credit for introducing policies and procedures which moved the Board and the Convention into the modern world.

Ernest Hollaway suggests the conclusion to this chapter:

> Have you ever watched the widening circle of ripples after you tossed a stone into a pond or a lake?. . . . Have you thought what might happen to the ripples if you tossed the stone into the mighty Pacific Ocean instead of into a pond? The small waves created by the stone would soon be lost amid the vast currents and sweeping tides of this huge body of water. But the influence of a man may be felt around the world—in spite of the fact that his influence is only one among many millions! Gaines S. Dobbins has exerted such an influence (*Baptist Training Union Magazine*, Oct. 1966).

4
Teacher (I)

In May 1918, Dr. Dobbins was honored by his *alma mater,* Mississippi College, with the degree of Doctor of Divinity. In October, classified by the Sunday School Board as an essential employee, he was exempted from Selective Service. In April 1919, the circulation of *Home and Foreign Fields* reached 31,000, an increase of 6,000 in 30 months. In June, promoted to the headship of the "Missionary Department," Dr. Dobbins became an executive of the Board. In October he became the father of a third son, Austin, his biographer.

In 1920 Dr. Dobbins regarded himself as a fixture at the Board. He was, he thought, fulfilling God's will. Then, again by an outside agency, his life was suddenly changed. "In late April," he recalled:

I was working in the garden when my wife called me to the telepnone. "Long distance for you from Louisville."

"This is E. Y. Mullins, your former professor at the Seminary," the voice declared. "The Committee on Faculty has just nominated you to inaugurate the new Department of Practical Studies at the Seminary."

"Wait a minute, Dr. Mullins," I interrupted. "You must have the wrong man. Aren't you thinking that you are speaking to E. C. Dargan?" Dr. Dargan at one time had been a professor at the Seminary.

"Oh, no," he said. "I have the right man. I've talked to Dr. Van Ness about your coming. [Actually Dr. Van Ness was responsible for the invitation.] He is reluctant to give you up, but we want to continue the tie that Landrum Leavell started here when he came as interim [1915-20] to teach about the Sunday School. We want the field broadened to include Church Administration." He called it "the Efficient Church." "You may retain your editorship. I'll expect you in my office at 10 o'clock Tuesday morning. It may be that the Lord wants you to do this. We think he does."

Well, I sat down and almost cried. I said to my wife, "I'm not going to do it.

Not in my wildest dreams have I ever thought of myself as a Seminary professor—there with all of those scholars. I'm not the type. I'm happy here where I am with my Sunday School Board assignment. And there's a great future ahead for us."

"Of course you can do it!" she calmly assured me. "Don't be too hasty. If that's the Lord's will, we'll make it ours. I'd rather stay here, too, but 'whither thou goest I will go' " (*Zest for Living*, 1977; Dillard Tape, 1978).

He did not know that earlier Dr. Mullins had approached Dr. Rufus W. Weaver, president of Mercer University, and Dr. Jesse B. Weatherspoon, pastor of First Baptist Church, Winston-Salem, who had rejected the offer. (Dr. Weatherspoon joined the Faculty later, in 1929, as professor of homiletics and sociology.) On this thin thread, writes Dr. K. Stephen Combs, Jr., "The Course of Religious Education at the Southern Baptist Theological Seminary" (doctoral thesis, 1978), rested Dr. Dobbins' career as a teacher. If . . . if . . . Dr. Weaver or Dr. Weatherspoon had accepted Dr. Mullins' offer, Dr. Dobbins would have remained at the Sunday School Board, possibly to become Executive Secretary, certainly to earn respect and honor as a religious journalist. Chance? Providence?

Preferring to remain at the Sunday School Board, Dr. Dobbins was impelled to go to Southern. Professor of Church Efficiency (Church Administration) and Sunday School Pedagogy (Religious Education) at Southern Seminary! What did he know of these subjects? Both at Gloster and at New Albany one of his major problems had been his lack of knowledge of church administration. He knew a bit more about Sunday School work. Drawing upon his experiences as a pastor, in 1919-20 he had published a dozen articles on Sunday School organization for Intermediates. But experience scarcely was an adequate substitute for academic training. And at the Seminary six years earlier the subject had received little attention. If he moved to Louisville, his salary—$3,500 with a house and $4,000 without—would be two to three times the amount he was making at Nashville. But money wasn't everything. What should he do? He had been a successful editor, a field in which he had had ten years of training. Could he be a successful educator, a field in which he had had less than a year of experience, in 1908-09, at South Mississippi College?

Again he received an answer: Christian service is not a matter of individual preference. To follow Christ is to give oneself up to the will and power of God, without counting the cost, but counting oneself fortunate to be able to turn over control of one's life to God. ("Test his claims," Dr. Aven had advised him long ago. "They work!") As a Christian Gaines Dobbins had been saved for service, not for himself but for his Master. This was the concept he had accepted in 1913 when he had been ordained as a minister. As a follower of Christ he was "not to be ministered unto, but to minister." In May 1920, Dr. Dobbins resigned his editorship of *Home and Foreign Fields,* a resignation which at first was accepted but later rejected. Thus for 12 years, from 1920 through 1932, Dr. Dobbins was both editor of *Home and Foreign Fields* and professor of Church Efficiency and Sunday School Pedagogy at Southern Seminary.

"How was your first year as a Seminary professor?" Dr. Badgett Dillard asked Dr. Dobbins in 1978. His reply was,

> Disappointing—to both my students and myself. But I had the gumption of being frank with them. Many of the men were more experienced than I was. I took them into my confidence and asked them to help plan the courses, and they did. I didn't know how modern my method was.
>
> Somehow we came to the end of the session. We didn't have any literature. But I had carried my little hand mimeograph machine with me. Working night and day, reading and conferring, I prepared materials that I tried to make both scholarly and practical. From these materials came my first book, *The Efficient Church.* I was not particularly anxious to be an author, but I didn't have anything on a seminary level to teach! (Dillard Tape, 1978; Biography III, *c.* 1971).

In order to teach one must have textbooks—this was the philosophy of the Seminary. Yet apart from Frederick Agar's *Church Finance* (1915), *Church Officers* (1918), Arthur Flake's *Building a Standard Sunday School* (1919, 1922), Landrum Leavell's *Senior B.Y.P.U. Manual* (1922), B. W. Spilman's *The Convention Normal Manual* (1909, 1918), and several older books, adequate texts were unavailable. To provide material for his classes, Dr. Dobbins began to read voluminously. The bibliography of his first book, *The Efficient Church* (1923), lists 90 books, 49 of which were published in 1920-22, 20 of which he reviewed in the Seminary journal, *The Review and Expositor,* after he was called to the Seminary.

In later years Dr. Dobbins was affectionately called "Mr. Mimeograph" by his students. There was reason for this title, for, innovatively, beginning in 1920 he provided his classes with 50- to 150-page workbooks, revised each year, which contained assignments and extracts from his writing and reading. In addition he furnished numerous outlines and study guides. It is said that once in his class he asked, "What surprises you as you study Jesus as teacher?" A student replied, "That he somehow got along so well without a mimeograph machine" (Andrew B. Rawls Videotape, Southern Seminary, Sept. 1, 1970). To Dr. Dobbins use of the mimeograph was a necessity. Since few textbooks in Church Administration and Religious Education were adequate, he was forced either to require his students to buy numerous texts (the catalog lists 19 for his two courses in 1920) or to write his own. His procedure was to "write a chapter of a book, mimeograph it, and give it to the students" to obtain their reaction. "Will what I have suggested work, is it valid, is it too radical?" he asked (Dillard Tape, 1978). He did not require recitations, memorization, or outlining. Instead, through discussion he and his students learned from each other. The mimeographed material saved students money and, as well, furnished the basis for his later books.

As a neophyte professor in 1920-21, however, Dr. Dobbins was anything but certain of himself. Frustrated by what he considered his lack of accomplishment, at the end of his first year of teaching he offered Dr. Mullins his resignation. His explanation was, simply, that he lacked knowledge of his subject. For a year he had "fumbled" his way from class to class, a member of a faculty composed of Mullins, Robertson, Gardner, Sampey—those of whom he later wrote appreciatively in *Great Teachers Make a Difference* (1965). But Dr. Mullins refused to accept his resignation. "True," he declared,

> you [Dr. Dobbins] haven't done very well as a teacher, but we didn't expect you to at first. You had no precedent. If we called someone else he would be in the same situation you are. You can learn. We're going to have this department. That's certain. We'll help you to go elsewhere to learn from other schools what you need to learn. The students like you. The Lord needs you here (K. Stephen Combs Tape, Dec. 10, 1976; Dillard Tape, 1978).

Thus, seeking to learn, summer after summer from 1921-33, when his presence was not required in Nashville as editor of *Home and Foreign Fields,* and during his two sabbatical years (1924-25, 1932-33), Dr.

Dobbins went back to school—to Vanderbilt, Peabody, Columbia (MA, 1925), Union Theological Seminary, the University of Chicago, institutions where he could obtain the training he needed. His book *Can a Religious Democracy Survive?* (1941) represented a rewriting of his Ph.D. thesis (Chicago), a degree which he did not obtain. "When he discovered," wrote Dr. Sampey,

> that he was expected to criticize sharply the educational methods of Southern Baptists, he chose to make no formal application for his degree. Dr. Dobbins was thoroughly loyal to the principles and methods adopted by the Sunday School Board (*Memoirs*, original ms., 1947, ed. Dobbins).

Acceptance of the degree would have required revision of his thesis to qualify its conservative (Southern Baptist) point of view. This Dr. Dobbins refused to do.

Lack of adequate preparation of Southern Seminary students in the "practical" field, as it was called, was the reason Dr. Mullins had asked Dr. Dobbins to broaden the field of studies taught earlier by Dr. Byron DeMent, Dr. George B. Eager, Dr. Charles S. Gardner, and Dr. Landrum Leavell, or, more accurately, to inaugurate a new department. For 13 years, studying at five distinctly different institutions, Dr. Dobbins sought to obtain guidance for students who knew *what* to preach but lacked preparation in *how* to lead churches administratively.

In his courses, particularly in the courses taught at Columbia, Dr. Dobbins was exposed to modern educational theories. What is education? What motivates students to learn? How do they learn? How does religious education differ from secular education? What is effective teaching? These seminal questions Dr. Dobbins heard discussed (discussed, not lectured upon) by three of the most influential educators of the time, John Dewey, William H. Kilpatrick, and George Albert Coe. "It doesn't make any difference what they are teaching," Dr. Coe, Dr. Dobbins' faculty advisor, insisted. (Dewey was teaching mathematics, the subject in which Dr. Dobbins had received his lowest grade, a "C," at Mississippi College.) "You need to observe their methods and objectives, to study their personality and philosophy—not to imitate them but to find yourself and determine the course you will pursue in a lifetime of teaching."

Following Dr. Coe's advice, Dr. Dobbins says,

a new world opened up to me. . . . Dewey was an upsetting educational radical, with his insistence that school should be society in miniature, where learning is experience leading to more enriched experience, and where teaching is stimulation and guidance of experience in preparation of the learner to do better what he is going to have to do anyhow (*Great Teachers Make a Difference*, 1965).

Kilpatrick, the most popular teacher on "the hill," undertook to implement Dewey's philosophy in terms of practical classroom procedures. A Baptist, he did not hesitate to bring religion into the picture. "We send our children to school," he would say, "but the home, the church, the community, and their classmates educate them." His major thesis was that "learnings never occur singly." There are direct learnings, which many teachers emphasize exclusively; but always there are indirect or associated learnings which are often more important than "book learning" for the learner's happiness and success. In religion learning is not just Bible knowledge but, more, a philosophy of life, positive or negative, developed toward moral and spiritual values (*The Alabama Baptist,* July 30, 1970, original copy).

The central figure among these teachers was Coe himself. "The purpose of religious education," he insisted, "is to bring growing persons into an ever-increasing awareness of God in Christ as controlling the whole of life in all areas of human living. We are, therefore, not to teach *lessons*, but *persons*" (*Great Teachers*, 1965).

What tremendously exciting ideas! Perhaps they no longer are revolutionary, but in 1920-30 they represented a different concept of education. Christian education is

the systematic, critical examination and reconstruction of relations between persons, guided by Jesus' assumption that persons are of infinite worth, and by the hypothesis of the existence of God, the Great Valuer of Persons (Coe, *What Is Christian Education?* 1929, quoted by Dobbins in *Review and Expositor,* Jan. 1936).

The terms of Coe's definition may be criticized; yet its import is clear. If enriched experience is the most important aspect of education, then Christian education, which teaches of the saving relationship between Christ and man, should regard each participant in the learning process as an individual whose personality is sacred. To Dr. Dobbins the Columbia educationalists provided support for beliefs he had long held, vaguely, imprecisely. Particularly were their insights valuable to Baptists, who tended to gloss over the influence of society upon the individual. What causes an individual to act as he does? In part his reactions are determined by pressures within his society.

Families are constantly moving, home life is weakened, moral standards fluctuate, temptations are multiplied, class and social lines are sharply drawn. Lodges, clubs, business and social organizations, community welfare organizations, commercialized amusements, all tend to complicate the work of the church. Specialization in employment, the reduction of life to schedule and routine, the struggle for a livelihood and to keep up appearances, the fact of unemployment, the extremes of wealth and poverty—these are not all new problems, but they present new phases and demand new effort at solution. What is bound to happen if church leaders and workers are incapable of meeting and coping with these difficult situations? (*The Efficient Church*, 1923).

In a complex society the church cannot exist as an island, isolated from the community. Instead it is a society which is part of a larger society, an interrelated community in which its members, young and old alike, respond differently to different stimuli. For learning to be effective, then, insisted Dewey, Kilpatrick, and Coe, the educator must recognize these stimuli. He must begin *where the pupil is.*

Interest must be aroused to the point that the learner is ready and eager to respond. If such readiness is lacking, to force the pupil to respond is to arouse an opposite mind-set, or antagonism, which may result in learnings that will actually be hurtful, even though the theme under discussion may be high and holy (*Working with Intermediates*, 1926).

Attach satisfaction to a response and it tends to be more readily learned; attach annoyance and it tends to drop out. People may continue to attend a Sunday school class in which they have no sense of satisfaction, but it is quite certain that they will learn practically nothing. The application of this law demands that the class period be so planned as to give genuine enjoyment; it means that comfortable and pleasing quarters will be provided so far as possible; it requires that the group shall be congenial, consisting of those who by reason of age and sex have interests in common; it requires that the teacher will seek for enjoyment, profit, helpfulness, increased understanding, deepened insight, enlarged powers to think and give expression to one's thoughts, changed attitudes and conduct that will make life sweeter and happier, strengthening the Christian life and helping to bring in the kingdom of God (*How to Teach Young People and Adults in the Sunday School*, 1930).

Interest, satisfaction, response. Life-enriching experiences (effective teaching) require Spirit-led guidance, careful preparation, appealing surroundings, adequate equipment, effective organization, recognition of the needs of the individual, in short, the following of Matthew 22:37-39 ("the first and great commandment. And the second is like unto it"). To the religious aspects of this sentence Dewey would have objected; but Kilpatrick and Coe would have agreed: Love of God leads to love of one's neighbor. Love of neighbor leads to satisfaction of needs. Satisfaction of needs leads to love of God. Love of God leads to. . . . Christ completes the circle.

Regarded as a master teacher in his later years, initially Dr. Dobbins lacked both the experience and the knowledge that are required for effective teaching. He became a great teacher by learning how to teach. Quotations (above) from three of his early books indicate that he was indebted to Dewey, Kilpatrick, and Coe, whose insights he used to raise the contents of his courses to graduate or seminary level. He was not an imitator, however. "I have never worn any man's educational collar," he remarked in 1950. His evaluation of himself was accurate. To Dr. Dobbins, although enticing, Dewey's educational system was too pragmatic, too little concerned with religion, to be used without qualification. Kilpatrick brought Christianity into the classroom, but his views, while valuable, were too experiential and, again, too pragmatic, to be accepted without reservation. Even Coe might be faulted for being overly concerned with the social aspects of the gospel. Instead of belonging to a particular "school" or group, Dr. Dobbins sought to be selective (eclectic).

Thus the pages of Dr. Dobbins' first nine books (1923-33) contain references not only to the views of Dewey, Kilpatrick, and Coe but also to those of Anton Boisen, Harrison Elliott, Edward L. Thorndike, under whom he studied, as well as to George H. Betts, William C. Bower, E. J. Chave, Luther Weigle, and other educationalists of the period. As a result, states Dr. Wayne Oates, Dr. Dobbins deliberately enlarged "the resources upon which a student could draw. He let no artificial lines of geography, denomination, or profession keep his student from the best leadership available in studying a problem" (*Great Teachers,* 1965). To Dr. Dobbins, knowledge was based upon ideas drawn from many fields of study.

It was partially this view which led Dr. Dobbins and Dr. Mullins to establish the March Pastor's Conference in 1929. In the '20s, in some respects Southern was deficient not only in its methodology but in its curriculum as well. Adherence to a transmissive theory of education was in part responsible. Inbreeding of the faculty also was a factor. Although they had studied at other institutions, each of the 11 members of the faculty had received his theological education at Southern. The March Conferences, which were designed to enlarge the academic horizons of the students, enriched the academic backgrounds, then, of the professors as well as the students. For two weeks each spring the Seminary family was enthralled (and sometimes horrified) with the viewpoints of such noted figures as Ellis Fuller (1929), Edwin B. Frost (1931), Carter Helm Jones (1934), Toyohiko Kagawa (1936), Roland Q. Leavell (1939), William Lyon Phelps (1942), John S. Bonnell (1945), and many others. To Dr. Dobbins, along with his other duties, fell the responsibility of directing the conferences.

Two additional "man-made" sources should be mentioned as being basic in the development of what Dr. Dobbins' students later called "Dobbinology," the key ideas which Dr. Dobbins presented to more than 12,000 students during the 49 years of his teaching ministry. His basic source was the Bible. So far as secondary sources are concerned, however, of numerous interwoven threads, three are particularly important.

First, the views of the Columbia educationalists.

Second, communication theory. In a number of ways Dr. Dobbins' ideas restated journalistic principles in terms of religious education and church administration. If the phrases "writing for Christian publications" and "the writer" referred to in chapter 3 are replaced with "practice of effective administration" and "the pastor," little else needs changing to restate the principles which inform Dr. Dobbins' early efforts to define the nature of a smoothly functioning or efficient church.

Third, efficiency engineering. The concept of "the efficient church" it is said Dr. Dobbins derived from his study of the writings of the efficiency experts in the field of business. According to Dr. Allen W. Graves, second dean of the School of Religious Education at Southern Seminary (1956-69, 1976-80),

> The emphasis upon efficiency that made such an impact on business and industry in America in the early decades of the twentieth century made a significant impact on the thinking of the young professor. His first book title [*The Effi-*

cient Church] reflects that impact (*Review and Expositor*, July 1978).

Dr. Graves' observation, which in part is based on a doctoral study of the subject by James L. Ryan ("A Study of the Administrative Theory of Gaines Stanley Dobbins in Relationship to the Scientific Management, Human Relations, and Social Sciences Emphasis in Administration," 1973), unquestionably is valid. In two of his early works, *The Efficient Church* (1923) and *Baptist Churches in Action* (1929), Dr. Dobbins readily acknowledged his indebtedness to Harrington Emerson's *Twelve Principles of Efficiency* (1910), Frederick W. Taylor's *Principles of Scientific Management* (1911), and Roger W. Babson's *Religion and Business* (1920), *New Tasks for Old Churches* (1922). Early in his professorship, he said,

I found that approaching the subject of Administration from the standpoint of the efficiency engineer appealed to the students and held their attention. The efficiency experts were beginning to create a reputable literature in their field. I got hold of some of the literature, Emerson's famous *Twelve Principles of Efficiency* and other books. I saw at once the relationship between the scholarly work and the courses in business administration that were being developed at Harvard, Yale, Princeton, Columbia, and elsewhere. At Vanderbilt and Peabody I examined how a university and a teachers' college got students ready for their jobs. My assumption was that a minister has a vocation. Preaching is involved, but not only preaching. A minister is the pastor of a church, an administrator. Out of my study grew my first effort at a book, *The Efficient Church*.

This little anecdote might be interesting. Dr. Mullins called me in [before I began teaching]. "This school is too content centered," he said. "We want it to be more closely tied in with the churches and we want to turn out men who have more practical experience. I have a vision, and the trustees have backed me up, of a new department that will be a new departure in seminary education. We want to establish a Department of Practical Theology."

Then he took off his glasses in characteristic fashion, looked at me quizzically and said, "I don't like that title. I teach theology and I think what I teach is practical." I replied, "Let's find a better name for it. I don't like it either. It isn't theology in the real sense of the word and it isn't just practicality." So we hit on the idea of calling it "Church Efficiency" and it went by that title for the first few years (Elmer L. Gray Tape, April 13, 1964; Combs Tape, 1976; Betsy Fleenor Tape, May 14, 1977).

To Dr. Dobbins, the concept of efficiency offered a practical means of solving problems in church administration. Efficiency as conceived in business is, of course, a secular concept. To Dr. Dobbins this was not necessarily a negative criticism. Truth may be fragmented into parts. Ideally, however, truth is a whole which is composed of interrelated parts. Thus he rejected the view that there were two types of efficiency, one which applied to business and another which applied to the church; two types of education, one which was secular, the other which was religious; two types of communication, one journalistic, the other ecclesiastic. To Dr. Dobbins, no conflict existed between business truth (if it is truth) and biblical truth. Actually, he said, the church is a business, Christ's business, in which the pastor as administrator is responsible for releasing the power of his flock as effectively and as efficiently as possible.

To release this power, following biblical principles, Dr. Dobbins proposed use of parallel principles advocated by Emerson in his *Twelve Principles of Efficiency*. What were these principles?

(1) *Clearly Defined Ideals* (Matt. 6:19-34; 7:24-27).

(2) *Common Sense* (Matt. 8:1-13; 12:1-14; 22:15-22).

(3) *Competent Counsel* (Gen. 41; Num. 10:29-32; 13; 2 Sam. 17; Acts 11).

(4) *Discipline* (Matt. 10:34-39; Luke 14:26-35; John 21:15-19; Rom. 16:17-20; 1 Cor. 5:9-13; 2 Thess. 3:6).

(5) *The Fair Deal* (Matt. 7:12; 18:1-5; Mark 9:33-37; Luke 9:46-48).

(6) *Records* (Isa. 40:12; Matt. 5:48; Luke 6:38; Eph. 4:13; 2 Cor. 10:12,13.

(7) *Dispatching* (Prov. 27:1; Matt. 8:21,22,24; 25:2-13; Acts 24:25).

(8) *Standards and Schedules* (Ex. 20; Matt. 20:18-20; Acts 1:8).

(9) *Standardized Conditions* (Gen. 1; 1 Kings 5; Acts 6:1-7).

(10) *Standardized Operations* (1 Cor. 14:40; 12:30).

(11) *Standard-Practice Instruction* (Deut. 4:1,2; 1 Cor. 14; 2 Tim. 2:1-15).

(12) *Efficiency Rewards* (Lev. 26:3-13; Matt. 10:30; 16:24-27; 20:1-16; 25:34-35; Luke 6:22, 23; Rev. 2:10) (Summarized from *The Efficient Church*, 1923, and *Baptist Churches in Action*, 1929).

In terminology the principles listed above are outmoded. As prerequisites for efficiency, however, they are still relevant. The need for their application in the '20s (in the '80s?) becomes evident if they are projected against the picture of the "average" Baptist church as it existed at the time. Study of this church (the "great majority of our churches," Dr. Dobbins wrote in 1929) revealed distressing conditions:

undeveloped spiritual resources, the over-worked few and the under-worked many, the idle capital tied up in seldom-used buildings, the uninformed and unenlisted majority, the poorly equipped educational plant, the under-paid and over-worked pastor.

Given these conditions, Dr. Dobbins insisted, something needed to be done. Churches might continue to stumble along without attaining maximum fruitfulness. But inefficiency is not God's plan. Efficiency is. To advance the cause of Christ requires use of means and methods which produce the best results. According to the educational theorists, inadequate methods block satisfaction and response. Of what value, Dr. Dobbins asked, is this knowledge if it is not applied? Failure to use efficient means (ideals of Christian love, willingness to serve, recognition of the needs of others) impairs the Christian cause. Similarly, failure to use efficient methods (including commonsense goals, effective standards, adequate records, appealing equipment, the concomitants of means) reduces the effectiveness of the Christian appeal. How best advance the cause of Christ? Surely by recognizing that efficiency is a spiritual as well as a secular concept. Means should not be separated from methods. Each leads to the same goal: "the best product in shortest time with least waste and greatest profit."

As a young professor Dr. Dobbins was surprisingly fresh and innovative in his teaching. That he was not alone among his colleagues in recognizing the value of efficiency engineering, however, is indicated by studies published by other religious educators, by H. F. Cope, *Efficiency in the Sunday School* (1912), Albert F. McGarrah, *Modern Church Management* (1917), Frederick Agar, *Democracy and the Church* (1919), and, particularly, Arthur Flake, *Building a Standard Sunday School* (1919, 1922), books which Dr. Dobbins knew and used. Cope and Agar were Northern Baptists. Flake was a Southern Baptist. The only book that was "at all relevant to what 'they' were calling on me to do," said Dr. Dobbins, was the book by Arthur Flake (Dillard Tape, 1978). Thus actually it was from Flake that Dr. Dobbins derived his orientation in efficiency as much as from Emerson, Taylor, or Babson. In Part I of *Building a Standard Sunday School,* Flake posited "two Standards by which Sunday Schools measure their efficiency." Part II considered methods and plans "for building an efficient Sunday School." In *Building a Standard Sunday School,* a book which is largely a text in business administration, Arthur Flake advocated a "Five-Step Formula for Building a Sunday School" which he based upon techniques which had been developed by Sears and Roebuck.

Step I. Take a census (Analyze your market).
Step II. Secure and train teachers and officers (Enlarge your organization).
Step III. Prepare adequate housing and equipment (Enlarge your store).
Step IV. Departmentalize and teach pupils according to their age and sex (Rearrange your stock).
Step V. Visit, visit, visit! (Obtain orders).

Each of the ten standards of the Standard of Excellence (Is it really so outdated?) fits into one or more of these steps.

In 1920, during the period in which Dr. Dobbins resided in Nashville, Mr. Flake was named secretary of the Department of Sunday School Administration at the Sunday School Board. Earlier, for 11 years (1909-20) he had traveled throughout the territory of the Convention, preaching his doctrine of efficiency. Flake's use of business techniques caught Dr. Dobbins' interest—as it did almost every Southern Baptist's. Here was a simple plan, yet, as Dr. Burroughs stated, "It had in it enough dynamite to blow up the Sunday School world and rebuild it on new lines." Could these techniques be applied to the church as a whole? To this question Dr. Dobbins began to seek an answer in his classes at Southern Seminary.

In 1920, using students from the Seminary and members of Walnut Street Baptist Church as workers, Dr. Dobbins conducted the first city-wide Sunday School census ever held in Louisville (Step I. Analyze your market.) In 1920 and in the years following Walnut Street embarked upon an extensive program of teacher training. (Step II. Enlarge your organization.) At Walnut Street the Sunday School was organized according to the traditional pattern—large "Baraca-Philathea" classes for adults, a class for children under twelve, two classes for Juniors, two for Intermediates, two for Young People. According to Flake (Step IV), Sunday Schools should be organized departmentally, not as single-class units. Departmentalization requires teacher-training.

A weekly meeting seemed to be the answer. A committee was appointed and plans were formulated. The pastor [Dr. Finley Gibson, a follower of Flake] announced and endorsed the project. Time for the first meeting came. The only ones present were the pastor and I and members of the committee. Undaunted, we tried again, this time through a person-to-person effort to explain and enlist. Soon the meeting became the center of our planning (*The Sunday School Builder,* Jan. 1969).

Effective administration requires leadership by the pastor. No less important is involvement by the laity. Why, of course! In a Baptist church ("a spiritual democracy"), the minister is an *episkopos,* a supervisor, a leader of leaders who has multiple responsibilities. "The pastor depends on his people, and the people upon their pastor; and the progress of the kingdom depends upon both" (*The Sunday School Builder,* Oct. 1920; reprinted Sept. 1970). Without lay participation, administration is largely fruitless.

In 1922, as a result of acting upon methods advocated by Dr. Dobbins, Walnut Street reported that Sunday School attendance "had increased from 450 to more than 900, the church auditorium no longer seated the congregation, financing of the church had increased, and the Training Union, which had been almost nothing, had begun to take on new life" (*Western Recorder,* May 4, 1922; Gray Tape, 1964; *Good News To Change Lives,* 1976). Broadway (1923), Tabernacle (1924), Clifton (1925), New Salem (1926), Crescent Hill (1928), and other Louisville area churches reported similar experiences. The methods advocated by Patterson, Van Ness, Coe, Emerson, Flake—in short, "Dobbinology," produced results.

Walnut Street Baptist Church, Louisville, became Dr. Dobbins' first testimonial as to what effective methods of church administration and religious education can do to vitalize a church. Since 1920 it has been a testimonial that has been repeated many times—at Washington, Richmond, Morganton, Ridgecrest, Greenville, Pensacola, Macon, Nashville, Dayton, St. Louis, Little Rock, Birmingham, Jackson, Macon, Monroe, San Antonio, Tulsa, Glorieta, Modesto, Portland, indeed, throughout the Convention. For over 50 years, in more than 110 churches Dr. Dobbins conducted week-long Leadership (Sunday School/Church) Clinics designed to persuade churches to apply the principles which formed the basis of his writing and teaching. Necessarily, since the problems of each church were different, in his clinics Dr. Dobbins followed no set pattern. A letter to Melvin Roberts, minister of education at First Baptist Church, San Antonio, indicates the nature of his approach, however. "My contribution, if any," he wrote,

> is made not through a series of lectures or mere discussions, but by getting down to "brass tacks" in the self-discovery of assets and liabilities—what you now have, wherein the present plans are adequate and inadequate, what you need immediately and ultimately, what changes will be necessary in order to meet these needs, difficulties in the way that must be dealt with carefully, means at your disposal for effective improvement, month by month procedures in carrying out plans agreed upon by your leadership. You can get plenty of people to make "talks" on Sunday School work—mine is an *engineering* [italics added] job that looks toward actual change and visible results. I shall want to prepare very carefully forms for study and checking, send them to you well in advance for mimeographing, and then have you place them in the hands of the right people who will take the project seriously (Letter, October 15, 1948).

Forged on the twin anvils of experience and scholarship, the principles Dr. Dobbins taught would suggest effective methods of approach. He would furnish guidance. The church would study itself.

A clinic, according to Webster, is a "group meeting devoted to the analysis and solution of concrete problems." Through group discussion, Dr. Dobbins sought to lead a church to examine its total resources. To provide the basis for the examination, he prepared check sheets (mimeographed, of course), lists of proposals, suggestions for discussion, and statements of difficulties. From data compiled from these sheets he drew his topics of discussion. According to outlines of discussions which he led at 33 clinics from 1943 to 1968, in a "typical" clinic Dr. Dobbins discussed some nine topics:

The Church Meeting the Challenge of Change
The Teacher Examining His Purpose
Understanding Those Whom We Teach
Teaching Seeks Fulfillment of Needs
Lesson Plans and Lesson Planning
Better Methods for Better Teaching
Jesus as Teacher
Helping Teachers to Evaluate Teaching
Church Progress Through Planning

At the end of the week Dr. Dobbins prepared an 8-10 page "Summary of Suggestions and Recommendations" for further study by each church. (Would that someone would pick up his mantle.)

For half a century, in individual churches as well as at Ridgecrest and Glorieta (1927-1969), Dr. Dobbins led clinics and conferences on the need for efficiency in advancing the cause of Christ. In his classes at Ridgecrest and Glorieta, which were popularized versions of his church clinics, through his courses at Southern, and by means of his writing, Dr. Dobbins emphasized a single theme: the necessity for effective leadership in the churches. When asked, "What is the church's greatest need?" stated Dr. Dobbins in *Learning to Lead* (1968), for 48 years pastors and lay leaders invariably replied: "consecrated, competent, conscientious leadership." In his "field work" in the churches Dr. Dobbins sought to supply this leadership. Because he provided what the churches needed, he became one of the most popular conference leaders in the South.

As a result, wrote Dr. R. Paul Caudill, through his efforts Dr. Dobbins, "more than any other living man, helped to determine the course of religious education in the churches of the Southern Baptist Convention" (Letter, Feb. 8, 1956). Similarly, stated Dr. Clifton J. Allen, "It is doubtful whether any other person has done so much as Dr. Gaines Dobbins to lift the level of Bible teaching among Baptists around the world" (*Baptist Training Union Magazine,* Oct. 1966). Again, declared Dr. Harper Shannon, "Dr. Dobbins' life and ministry have touched untold numbers of people through the years. My life has been one of those positively affected for God and for good because of his influence" (Letter, July 6, 1976).

The statements might be multiplied indefinitely.

5
Teacher (II)

In 1967 Dr. Dobbins wrote an article titled "50 Years of Church Administration as I Have Seen It Unfold." In this article he classified the fifty years from 1920 to 1970 into four periods or decades, I. The Decade of Standardization, 1920-30, II. The Decade of Organizational Complexity, 1930-40, III. The Decade of Correlation and Specialization, 1940-50, and IV. The Decade of Adjustment and Renewed Outreach, 1960-70 (*Church Administration,* Dec. 1967). In that it omits the Decade from 1950-60, the classification is not wholly accurate. Yet it is useful in that it indicates Dr. Dobbins' significance as an educator for fifty crucial years of the twentieth century. The history of Dr. Dobbins' endeavors during this period was not identical, of course, with that of the Convention. Nevertheless, using one of Dr. Dobbins' favorite words, between the two there was a close correlation.

I. *The Decade of Standardization, 1920-30.* In the decade of the '20s, writes Dr. Allen W. Graves, church leaders throughout the South looked for the "best way of administering church affairs and sought to develop standards that would assure efficiency and desired results" (*Review and Expositor*, July 1978). Does standardization produce desired results? To this question, in 1920 business leaders, government officials, and educators, as well as, apparently, the public in general had little doubt as to the answer. As a result of standardization, automobiles were produced, cheaply and effectively; war material was manufactured, with efficient, interchangeable parts; the gross national product rose from $20,000,000,000 in 1900 to almost $90,000,000,000 in 1920. Responding to as well as leading Southern Baptists in their desire for standardization, in *Baptist Churches in Action* (1929) Dr. Dobbins printed six "Standards of Excellence," to generalize their titles, for the Sunday School, Associational Sunday School, Baptist Young People's

Union, Senior Baptist Young People's Union, Woman's Missionary Union, Brotherhood (Laymen's Missionary Movement), as well as a "Constitution" for the church as a whole. Each of the "Standards" had been developed by Southern Baptist agencies before 1929. Earlier, in 1925, the acceptance by the Convention of a "Cooperative Program" and a regularized, although noncredal, "Baptist Faith and Message" indicated further recognition by Southern Baptists of their need for standardization.

Yet the view was by no means universal. Baptists being Baptists, not all Southern Baptists approved of the application of methods of efficiency to denominational life. Criticism from adherents to Landmarkism was to be expected. More surprisingly, objection to the "substitution" of courses in method for courses solidly founded on the Bible was voiced by Dr. Dobbins' colleagues as well. At an early faculty meeting, Dr. Dobbins recalled,

> after I had made an announcement about some work we were undertaking, one very notable member of the faculty responded, "I don't go for this. A student has three years in which to get the fundamentals of a theological education. If I had my way we would somehow endow these students. I could wish that he would do nothing except his classwork, not even preach on Sunday, in order that he might give his full attention to getting the framework of a scholarly, theological education" (Gray Tape, 1964).

In addition to Greek and Hebrew, history and theology, the classical disciplines, Dr. Dobbins proposed that students study the church, its community, its methods and organizations, its standards and goals. While academically interesting, perhaps, said his critics, these subjects scarcely were suitable objects of scholarly study.

In 1920-30, as a number of students observed openly, the Seminary was considerably behind the times in its methods of instruction. Recognition of this deficiency was Convention-wide. In 1917, responding to a resolution passed by the Convention in 1916, the Sunday School Board had published a manual which called upon the seminaries to establish a "Chair of Baptist Church Administration." One of the most serious deficiencies in seminary education, stated the manual, is that

> we have left almost wholly untouched that field in which the modern pastor finds his greatest problems and difficulties. We have been satisfied to give our preachers a literary and theological training, and to send them forth amidst the

many-sided problems of the modern pastorate without even so much as a definite course of lectures on Church Finances, and the other important business and organization problems which they must immediately meet when they find themselves the leaders of the church. The greatest occasion for pastoral unrest and unhappiness does not arise out of an inadequate literary and theological culture but out of a deficiency of knowledge and ability to deal with the business and organization side of pastoral leadership (*Church Organization and Methods*, 1917, by Selsus E. Tull, Lansing Burrows, and others).

Southern was not the only seminary which was scolded by the Convention. The criticism applied to Southwestern as well. In fact, during the '20s theological schools in general questioned the value of the "practical" approach to education.

At Southern, recognizing the need of the churches, Dr. Mullins determined to establish a department of church efficiency and Sunday School pedagogy. The faculty, however, was not completely convinced of the wisdom of the decision. Although deeply disturbed, Dr. Dobbins made no overt response to criticism of his field. Instead, giving credit to others, in his writing and in his classes, quietly and uncontroversially he presented the biblical bases for studying organization and method. "God, who is Life," he wrote in *The Efficient Church* (1923),

is the Great Organizer. Nothing that man may ever do can compare with his infinite genius for organization who created the heavens and the earth, and who from the planetary system to the microscopic atom has arranged in perfect order all things in his universe. God seems to have done all things, and continues to do all things, through the perfection of divine organization. Christ organized the twelve apostles, and the seventy; he displayed divine wisdom in relating his followers to himself, to each other, and to the work which he intended for them to do. . . . We go with the divine current when we work through and by means of organization. The pastor or Christian worker who would follow after God and his Son and the great workers whom God and Christ have used in the redemptive plan must understand the motive and value of organization.

"Be ye therefore perfect, even as your Father in heaven is perfect," is the standard of Jesus. It is not enough to say that such a standard is unattainable. It is the flying goal toward which *every Christian* should strive, even though its final attainment must wait upon eternity. . . . The efficient church, measuring up to the New Testament ideal, is an "every-member" church, and will never be satisfied until all its members "attain unto the unity of the faith, and of the knowledge of the Son of God, unto a full grown man, unto the measure of the stature of the fullness of Christ." This ideal may never be fully reached but no other ideal is worthy of Christ and his kingdom (*Baptist Churches in Action*, 1929).

God is the Great Organizer. Christ believed in standards. The purpose of organization and standards (church administration and religious education) is to bring individuals to God through Christ. With this point of view it was difficult to argue. Moreover, both in his teaching and in his writing Dr. Dobbins recognized the value of the classical disciplines. He maintained the historic Baptist emphasis upon preaching as the central exercise of the church. Acknowledging that "what will work in one community may be utterly impracticable in another," he recognized that "organization is never an end in itself" (*The Efficient Church*). Nevertheless, he refused to accept the view that study of method and organization, the practical discipline, was less important than study of biblical languages and interpretation. To the contrary, he insisted that "teaching and training agencies are not incidental in the work of the church; they are absolutely essential." Christ admonished, "As the Father sent me, even so send I you." Thus

the missionary spirit, the evangelistic spirit, are both the spirit of highest service; ministries of teaching, of healing, of comforting, of caring for the unfortunate and needy, of creating and maintaining a better social order, all are forms of service which represent Christianity in action, and are an integral part of the program of Jesus for the establishment of his kingdom upon the earth (*Baptist Churches in Action*).

Preaching remains the minister's first responsibility. But preaching involves more than conducting a worship service. Preaching involves witnessing, the primary responsibility of every Christian. Witnessing involves use of the total resources of the church—the Sunday School, Training Union, Woman's Missionary Union, Brotherhood, the Church Council, the deacons—each of the organizations of the church. "Go . . . preach . . . make disciples . . . baptize . . . teaching them." The goals of church administration (including religious education), then, are the goals of every pastor: "To develop soul-winning personal workers in the ranks of the laity who will make possible the apostolic ideal of adding unto the church day by day those that are saved" ("Inaugural Address," *Review and Expositor*, Oct. 1920).

II. *The Decade of Organizational Complexity, 1930-40*. In 1920 church administration was a relatively simple field of study. The problem that faced pastors during the "Age of Complexity" was largely that church administration (the generic term) now was too varied, too diverse, too complex for the average minister to grasp. In 1920 there were few textbooks in administration. By 1940, as a result of the recognition of its value by most of the American denominations, there were multitudinous texts in the field. Cited most frequently by Dr. Dobbins were texts by W. P. Phillips, *The Adult Department of the Sunday School* (1930), Paul H. Vieth, *Objectives in Religious Education* (1930), J. M. Price, *Introduction to Religious Education* (1932), P. E. Burroughs, *How to Win to Christ* (1934), Ordway Tead, *The Art of Leadership* (1934), Ernest Chave, *Personality Development in Children* (1937), John S. Bonnell, *Pastoral Psychiatry* (1938), Rollo May, *The Art of Counseling* (1939), and A. W. Palmer, *The Art of Conducting Public Worship* (1939). To these studies might well be added an additional 100, each of which suggests another, and still another, field of interest.

As an infant grows from simple to complex responses, similarly, from 1920 to 1940, the field of administration developed from childhood to adolescence. In its second decade, according to the writers of the texts, competency in church administration required the administrator to be a biblical scholar, a teacher, counselor, psychologist, sociologist, and political scientist. He was expected to be an effective public speaker, motivator, bookkeeper, and (at least occasionally, assuming that he was married) a husband and provider for his family. Arguing that their function was to minister, not administer, some students responded to the demands of administration with resentment. Popularly, Dr. Dobbins' course in "Principles and Methods" ("P. and M.") was referred to as "Pain and Misery!"

In part the reference was jesting; it also indicated a belief that courses in methods required too much work. Expressing an opposite point of view, other students, said Dr. Dobbins, became so enamored with administrative theory that they "weakened the spiritual ministries of the church, substituting method for the Holy Spirit of God" (Gray Tape, 1964). In 1934, addressing the students at the September opening of the Seminary, Dr. Dobbins proposed a more balanced approach. What training does a minister need, he asked, if he is effectively to meet the demands which are made upon his time? "First," he suggested, the successful minister of today and tomorrow muct be *equipped for critical thinking on the basis of broad and accurate scholarship*. Never was the temptation to superficiality greater than now. Greek and Hebrew are difficult, and translations of the Scriptures abound. Why spend precious time reading the Bible in the original? Sermon outlines, and even complete sermons ready for delivery, may be had cheap for cash. . . . Theology is out of date, psychology is a delusion, sociology a snare, missions an outmoded and impractical dream, church organization and administration a thorn in the flesh, religious education an invention of the devil and the modernists. Thus the minister may reason with himself, and go out to do nothing but "preach the gospel and win souls." Strangely enough, however, he soon finds himself with nothing to preach and no souls to save. The churches . . . skillfully pass the brother on when at the end of the year he has exhausted his available supply of sermons (*Review and Expositor*, April 1935).

All fields of learning contain difficulties. Whether the subject is Greek or church administration, the statement remains the same. It is exposure to these difficulties, leading to critical thinking, that makes education worthwhile. Not all of what is studied is valuable, but one must know the solutions which have been proposed before one can reach valid conclusions, based on Christ's teachings. Good teaching, Dr. Dobbins maintained, restating his fundamental law of education, produces stimulation which leads to satisfaction and response.

The statement probably did not accurately represent the educational theory held by the faculty at Southern in 1934. At the least, however, it presents a general view of Dobbins' methodology. Education requires, first, the ability to think critically. Critical thinking requires a knowledge of one's subject, derived from reading books, writing papers, and examining issues in class: What are the faults (if any) of Flake's formula for building successful Sunday Schools? What are the functions of (1) the Sunday School, (2) the Training Union, (3) the Woman's Missionary Union, (4) the Brotherhood? What is involved in an effective church program for children? How motivate young people and/or adults? What are the differences between a teaching church and an evangelistic church? Do these approaches necessarily conflict? Conclusions to these and other questions should be tested initially, Dr. Dobbins suggested, in the give-and-take of classroom discussion, then through the study of psychology and creative experience with individuals and groups.

Second, then, a minister should be "*equipped with a thorough understanding of human nature and conduct*."

Once the assumption was that students were to withdraw from the busy life of the world to acquire knowledge and ability which they would take with them when they re-entered human affairs. That assumption has been definitely proved fallacious. Men learn best what they have put to use; and scholarship is vitalized only by its contact with life. A student's usefulness may be seriously marred by bookishness divorced from human experience. Men may be actually miseducated who achieve the highest scholastic grades if there is failure to thrust them out into the current of the world's problems and needs. The by-products of three or more years of guided experience in a cosmopolitan student body at work in a great city may easily be worth as much as the formal classroom discipline (*Review and Expositor*, April 1935).

The "well-equipped" minister is a person who is able to apply critical thinking to human problems. This view Dr. Dobbins applied particularly to courses in church administration. On the one hand, a minister whose preaching is isolated from life is poorly educated (Aven, Patterson, Coe, Price, Burroughs, *et al*). On the other hand, a minister who regards administration primarily as a matter of statistics, surveys, and/or systems also is poorly trained. Neither adequately understands the nature of administration. What is administration? Properly defined, in terms used by Ordway Tead (*The Art of Leadership*, 1934), administration is "the activity of influencing people to cooperate toward some goal which they come to find is desirable" (Quoted by Dr. Dobbins in *Church Administration*, Dec. 1967). It is the art of the practical, an attempt to do effectively what should be done anyway. In part it deals with things (subject matter); it is concerned more vitally with subject matter examined critically and validated by experience with persons. Theory unrelated to persons is lifeless.

What follows? To Dr. Dobbins the answer to this question was clear: the necessity of determining (1) the goals which the minister as administrator will attempt to achieve, and (2) the goals which his constituency actually will support. As administrator a minister must be both an organizer and motivator. (Leadership . . . education . . . communication require response.) What activities does a congregation feel are desirable? Is a church composed of members who are wealthy, conservative, liberal, educated, indifferent, concerned, periodically or constantly evangelistic? What do surveys show about the community? Is the neighborhood industrialized, urban, rural, suburban? What "competition" is there? To answer these questions, Dr. Dobbins organized his classes into teams which worked with pastors of the local churches, studying church life and organization, conducting surveys, making charts and maps, working in hospitals, social agencies and other institutions, projecting plans for the future. Techniques of surveying and map-making may be learned from the study of books; understanding the relationship of a church to its community requires asking questions which can only be answered in terms of human response. To be sure, *vox populi* is not *vox dei*. Goals are set by the Bible, not by the community. Nevertheless, without knowledge of itself and its community it is difficult for a church to determine and to reach its goals.

To Dr. Dobbins, administration was not a field which prospective ministers might ignore or study at will. To lead, a minister must be an administrator. He must preach, but not in isolation from people. Yet, admittedly, since a minister's time is limited and humanity is complex, administrative theory is too complicated for the average minister. How can this problem be resolved? First, suggested Dr. Dobbins, by recognizing that administration is not as difficult as some have claimed. "Methods are many, although principles are few." "Standards" vary according to the community. With training, ministers of smaller churches should be able to respond to the administrative needs of their churches with a considerable degree of confidence. (Small does not mean little.) Second, by recognizing that ministers of larger churches need the assistance of specialists—associate pastors, ministers of education, of music, of administration, of counseling, and other areas. For these specialists, ordination might or might not be advisable. Actually, in a church in which witnessing is the task of everyone, leadership furnished by pastorally trained lay persons might be preferable to that furnished by the theologically trained minister.

In 1934, recognizing the need for specialization, Southern Seminary redefined the term "minister" to include persons "committed to the calling of Christian education although not purposing ordination to the pastoral ministry" (catalog statement). For this change Dr. Sampey, Dr. Carver, and Dr. Dobbins were largely responsible. In 1943 Southern initiated undergraduate and Master-level training for ministers of music with Bachelor of Divinity in Religious Education and Master of Religious Education programs for ministers of education following in 1948 and 1953. Doctoral programs were authorized in 1956. (It is difficult to realize how revolutionary specialized training was regarded by some in the '30s and '40s.) The Age of Complexity had arrived. The training of specialists alleviated the problems of the larger churches. The period left unresolved, however, the problems of effective administration in small churches and left behind an overorganized Convention, problems which received attention during the '40s, the period which Dr. Dobbins called—

III. *The Decade of Correlation and Specialization, 1940-50.* In 1845 the Southern Baptist Convention consisted of 4,395 churches with a membership of 365,316. Perhaps 500 Sunday Schools existed. Other organizations, such as the Woman's Missionary Union, Brotherhood, and Training Union were not established until 1888 (WMU) or later. In 1945 the Convention consisted of 26,134 churches with 5,865,554 members. Organizations included 24,968 Sunday Schools, 12,734 Woman's Missionary Unions, 3,300 Brotherhoods, and 11,736 Training Unions.

The figures would seem to represent a triumph for methodology and the application of standards. And they do. In the period from 1920 to 1945 increase in Southern Baptist membership was almost 200 percent greater than it had been from 1845 to 1920. What the figures do not reveal is that in 1945 the organizations of the church included numerous suborganizations, many of which existed with duplicate and overlapping programs. As a result, at the 1946 Convention, from overburdened pastors came a call to "Simplify, unify, eliminate duplications." Their problem was threefold: (1) Within the Convention, the denominational calendar permitted too many activities to be scheduled by the Convention agencies. (2) The agencies themselves scheduled activities which overlapped those of other agencies. And (3) In the smaller churches, particularly, leadership was unavailable to staff the programs. The result was wasted effort—and renewed objection to administrative complexity.

"There is always something going on in a Baptist church." The statement generally is made with a chuckle. The existence of organizations with overlapping functions frequently is not amusing to the minister, however. In the '40s, reacting against the overorganization brought about by the "Age of Complexity," pastors called for help. This was not the first time the call had been issued. In 1937 (and earlier, in 1914), messengers to the Convention had authorized a committee to study the problem. Unfortunately, the resolutions of the 1937 committee, of which Dr. Dobbins was a member, had produced few results. Dissatisfied, in 1946 messengers to the Convention again sought help. In part their request was sparked by an article written by Dr. Dobbins in 1939. In this article, drawing upon his experiences as a member of the 1937-42 committee, Dr. Dobbins asked a number of questions:

Have we too many intra-church organizations? Could some of them be combined to advantage? Should not their functions be more carefully defined and delimited? Can they not be more effectively related to one another and to the church? Have we not reached the place in our church development where we can calmly and dispassionately evaluate these several organizations, and so coordinate the activities in which they engage as to secure maximum efficiency for the church to which they belong? (*Review and Expositor*, Jan. 1939).

The quotation is taken from Dr. Dobbins' "Work Book for Religious Education" (September 1939), a syllabus designed to guide Seminary students to understand the organization of the Convention. The "Work Book" expressed a view which he had stated earlier, although less forcefully, in *The Efficient Church* (1923) and *Baptist Churches in Action* (1929). Other factors supported the call for change, of course. Upset due to World War II, dissatisfaction and objection to established methods, the failure of the Convention to make major structural changes since 1931—these and other factors led to a *demand* at the Miami Convention that the boards and agencies of the Convention organize themselves more efficiently.

To Dr. Dobbins as chairman of the 1946 Committee on Church Organizations (the "Committee on Coordination and Correlation") fell the task of guiding the reorganization. He could not direct. He had no mandate to make specific changes. "Never before in my life have I been confronted with an assignment as difficult and delicate," he wrote Dr. P. E. Burroughs, a Convention sponsor of the Committee.

I asked earnestly to be left off the committee, but my personal wishes were overlooked. . . . Beyond question there is a tidal wave of desire that the committee do something worthwhile. You and I know full well that there can be worked out no magic formula (Letter, July 1, 1947).

The problem that the Committee faced was a difficult one. It is said that the history of the Southern Baptist Convention is a history of two opposing tendencies, a desire for autonomy on the one hand and a desire for standardization (organization) on the other. Duplication of effort is bad. Is the creation of what might become a "super-board" better? The Sunday School Board, itself a super-board, questioned the need for change. The Woman's Missionary Union similarly expressed disapproval. At the first full meeting of the Committee (Feb. 2, 1947), wrote Dr. Dobbins, "It was cold in Memphis—sleet and snow covered the ground—but the reception given the committee was just about as frigid" (*Baptist History and Heritage*, July 1970). In May, at the St. Louis Convention, a resolution was introduced to dismiss the Committee. The response of the messengers was a resounding no. The next meeting of the Committee took place in a different atmosphere. In the words of Anonymous, "Mama [the Convention] had spoken." Something must be done about the numerous and overlapping programs—programs sponsored by orphanages, hospitals, educational institutions, Mission Boards, Sunday School, Woman's Missionary Union, Brotherhood—which churches were expected to administer Sunday after Sunday. Perhaps administrative simplicity could not be achieved, but something could be done.

In 1950 the report of the "Dobbins Committee," as it was sometimes called, was adopted by the Convention. The Committee sought no radical revision of Southern Baptist organization. This was not what the Convention wanted. According to questionnaires sent to 11,500 pastors and ministers of education throughout the Convention, what was desired was, simply, that the boards and agencies of the Convention adopt a correlated calendar of activities by standardizing its standards, eliminating (for example) duplicate appeals for funds and overlapping programs, reducing the number of meetings, and unifying the Bible-reading selections and study course requirements. The cost of compiling the questionnaire, it should be noted, was borne by the Sunday School Board, an agency which throughout its history has supplied funds for Convention causes. As a result of the work of the Committee,

1. A revised calendar of denominational activities was adopted. "For the first time in Southern Baptist history," Dr. Dobbins wrote, "representatives of the several boards and agencies met [at Memphis, 1947] to consider how they might work *together* in the interest of the churches" (Letter, Oct. 30, 1947).

2. Agreement was reached that new plans would not be initiated by one of the organizations without consultation with the others.

3. On the local level, the church council concept was approved. Decrease in frequency of organization meetings was recommended (25 per cent was a suggested figure). A beginning was made in modifying Bible reading requirements.

Provision of alternate programs was suggested for the approximately 15,000 churches which had fewer than 150 members.

4. On the denominational level, the Inter-Agency Council, a voluntary organization, was formed. Composed of representatives from the Sunday School Board, the Foreign Mission Board, the Home Mission Board, the Brotherhood, and the Woman's Missionary Union, since 1948 the Inter-Agency Council has functioned efficiently to reduce tension and promote organizational harmony within the Convention.

The recommendations of the 1946 Committee on Church Organizations were similar in nature to those presented by the 1937 Committee. Unlike the recommendations of the 1937 Committee, the proposals of the 1946 Committee, however, were acted upon—not wholly but in large part. It was not until 1958, with the report of the Committee to Study the Total Baptist Program, that organizational unity was achieved (to the extent that it has been achieved). Even today, provision by Convention agencies for alternate programs for churches with fewer than 150 members remains more of an ideal than a practice.

IV. *The Decade of Adjustment and Renewed Outreach, 1960-70.* In 1949, commenting on the Third Report of the Committee on Church Organizations, Dr. Dobbins suggested that the work of the sixteen members of the Committee marked

> an epoch in the life of our churches. Having gone from simplicity to complexity, we are now on our way back to a greater degree of New Testament simplicity. Having developed organizations once conceived of as apart from the denomination and churches, we now see all these organizations as integral parts of the whole, with the local church body a true unity (*Western Recorder*, May 5, 1949).

Dr. Dobbins' statement is puzzling if it is projected against the clouds of perplexity which enveloped America after the Second World War. In 1949 church life in the United States was more, not less, complex than it had been earlier. The statement contains meaning, however, if one recognizes that to Dr. Dobbins perhaps the most significant aspect of the work of the Committee on Organizations was its advocacy of the return to the New Testament concept of the church council. Through this council, he believed, control of Convention organizations could be restored to the local church.

Agencies and boards exist, Dr. Dobbins wrote, to provide churches with "the best materials, the most workable patterns of organization and administration, the most practical means of leadership training, the most useful standards for the setting up and attainment of desirable aims." Since churches function most fruitfully through teamwork, "the best way," as it is determined by the boards and organizations of the Convention—and by the Convention itself, ordinarily will be adopted by the individual churches. Yet "what will work in one community may be utterly impracticable in another" (*The Efficient Church*, 1923; *Review and Expositor*, April 1936; *Building Better Churches*, 1946; *The Churchbook*, 1951; *A Ministering Church*, 1960). "The most fascinating thing about life," he wrote in 1936,

> is its variety and modifiability, and teaching and learning become wooden and dull when reduced to the level of the mechanistic. No greater misfortune could overtake education than to discover and formulate the one "best method," as does an automobile factory, and then proceed to turn out intellectual factory products as alike as this year's Fords. Let us settle it with ourselves that there is not and should never be a single uniform "best method," be it new or old, but a variety of methods supported by certain sound principles that have stood the test of time, and that are meeting the demands of present living in a world as it is made up of people as they are (*Review and Expositor*, April 1936).

To Dr. Dobbins, methods were subordinate to life. Thus variations or adjustments, provided they did not conflict with Christian beliefs, were possible, even necessary, if the needs of the local churches were to be met. The New Testament solution to problems of adjustment (Acts 15) was the church council, composed of leaders of the church, who met regularly

> for consideration of the pastor's plans, for conference concerning the plans and schedules of the several organizations, for the ironing out of difficulties before they reach the acute stage, for the sharing of one another's problems, for the making of recommendations that will have back of them the strength of the whole church (*Building Better Churches*, 1947).

Divided into committees, the council would eliminate much of the complexity involved in administering the affairs of churches, both large and small.

It was in this sense, then, that Dr. Dobbins referred to the 1949 report of the Committee on Organizations as marking an epoch in Southern Baptist life. In methods, the "best way" is not always the only way.

Rather the best way provides for variations and adjustments. Standards exist, but, as was recognized by the agencies of the Convention, they exist in terms of people and ranges of choice. "Today's church," wrote Dr. Dobbins in 1967,

> will invite and attract all those it can to its services of worship, proclamation, education, and ministry, but it will with equal zeal seek to take its worship, message, and teaching to those who cannot or will not attend. The church will do its utmost to enrol and teach all it can reach in Sunday School, but it will take the Bible to those who do not come. The church will maintain at highest possible level a training service for its members, but it will extend its training program in many other ways beyond Sunday evening.
>
> The church will seek to engage its total membership in missionary concern and practice. The church will include a men's organization, but it will go further and seek to utilize its total manpower for the total church and denominational enterprise. The church will appreciate and approve its Music Ministry, but it will enlist the use of music in all that it undertakes within and without the church.
>
> Administration thus conceived will cease to be a burden to pastor, staff, church officers and other leaders, and will become a way of fulfilling their high calling. The minister will preach the gospel with greater power to larger congregations. The church organizations will function more smoothly and fruitfully. The staff members and church-elected leaders will pray and work together that they may enlist and nurture every member and extend the outreach of the church.
>
> Church administration thus conceived will not minimize tangible results but will magnify concern for persons (*Church Administration*, Dec. 1967).

To reach its constituency, a church must recognize the need for multiple ministries and alternate programs, programs which will follow alternate plans to reach the same goals. This is the view which informed the series of nine books which Dr. Dobbins published from 1950 to 1970. Does it represent a change in concept? Dr. James L. Ryan regards the development of Dr. Dobbins' ideas as a movement from a Scientific Management through a Human Relations to a Behavorial Science point of view (*Review and Expositor*, July 1978). Without arguing over terms, for these were labels which Dr. Dobbins both knew and used, perhaps a better description of Dr. Dobbins' variations in point of view is that they represent expansions and reemphases rather than movements from one ideology to another. The basic source of his ideas was the Bible. To this source he added study and personal experience, with study sometimes preceding, sometimes confirming experience. Unquestionably, as he grew older Dr. Dobbins became less rigid in his views. Nevertheless, in his ideology he was amazingly consistent. (Consistency does not mean inability to change.) As a Christian journalist, he advocated five principles (chapter 3), principles which basically were the same as those which he advocated as a teacher. Similarly, in *The Efficient Church,* his first book, he emphasized the need for standards. Yet standards, he insisted, are not ends in themselves.

> We cannot win the lost, build up the saved in Christian character, and project the influence of the church with passion and power by card indexes, filing systems, intricately organized auxiliary societies and church clubs, well-equipped buildings, effective financial systems, attractive advertising, or any other such agency, apart from regenerated, spiritually-minded, warm-hearted, passionately earnest men and women who have a genuine experience of grace. These agencies may indeed be made to serve spiritual ends, and the modern church should use them with intelligent discrimination, and even enthusiasm; but let us not deceive ourselves into thinking that we can bring in Christ's kingdom by management and device.
>
> To reach the goal of every-member enlistment the conception of the church's function must be enlarged. We must cease to think of the church as primarily an institution for preaching, where a congregation passively listens while the preacher delivers his message. Instead we must come back to Paul's conception of the church as the body of Christ, which, though having many members, is yet one body. For the young there must be provided activities and nurture suited to their years and capacity. Vigorous and mature men and women must be furnished spiritual food and exercise necessary to their strength and well-being. To the weak, the infirm, the aged, must be given the care and service that their condition demands.

People—people cared for and led to Christ through varying approaches—people are more important than methods and traditions.

Much the same outlook appears in the books written by Dr. Dobbins from 1950-1970. In these books, in which the language remains crisp and fresh, the vocabulary occasionally is unfamiliar. To readers of his earlier writings, Dr. Dobbins' use of such terms as "depth psychology," "interpersonal relations," "multiple ministries," "pastoral care," "secularism," "social activism," and "theology of hope" may have seemed a bit unusual. (The terms appear infrequently. Dr. Dobbins avoided jargon as much as possible.) The citations and footnote references, of course, also were different. But this was to be expected, for Dr. Dobbins constantly used fresh sources in all his writings, with the exception of one book. The old but always fresh, unchanged but still new book was the Bible.

It was this source that furnished the basis for the emphasis upon multiple approaches that distinguished Dr. Dobbins' later books from those which he had written earlier. Christ's ministry included teaching (Matt. 5:2), preaching (Mark 2:2), administration (Luke 10:1), healing (Matt. 4:23), counseling (Isa. 9:6)—multiple ministries combined in a single ministry. To fulfill this goal, since Christ's followers are limited, specialists might be required in the larger churches. Regardless of the size of the church, however, Dr. Dobbins believed, the concept of multiple approaches was essential if Christians were to achieve the goal of witnessing to every person. (Multiple approaches, person-mindedness, behavioral science techniques, *diakonia*, interdisciplinary concepts, pastoral care—the terms vary but the principles largely are the same. Currently the most popular term is pastoral care.)

Recognition of the need for pastoral care Dr. Dobbins found in the Bible. To implement this view he turned to the writings of students of human nature in the fields of theology, sociology, psychology, and medicine. Before 1940, aside from pioneering work by John Dewey, George Albert Coe, Anton Boisen, and Luther Weigle, there were few texts which sought to combine these disciplines into an organic whole. By 1959-60, including studies written by Dr. Dobbins and his students (Wayne Oates being the most prominent), a number of interdisciplinary texts had been published. In *Zest for Living* (1977), Dr. Dobbins cited nine studies which he regarded as being particularly useful and as being on a graduate level: Karl Menninger's *Man Against Himself* (1938), Lawrence Frank's *Human Conservation* (1943), Seward Hiltner's *Religion and Health* (1943), Carroll Wise's *Religion in Illness and Health* (1942), Carl Rogers' *Counseling and Psychotherapy* (1942), Karen Horney's *New Ways in Psychotherapy* (1939), Gordon Allport's *Personality: A Psychological Interpretation (1937)*, Russell Dick's *And Ye Visited Me* (1939), and Richard Cabot's *Art of Ministering to the Sick* (1938).

Actually the "sources" of pastoral care, an interdisciplinary concept, are not as important as the view of the ministry which it presents. On the one hand it leads to clinical work with those who are "lost" in hospitals, sanitoriums, jails, child-care centers, and other institutions. (The Association of Clinical Pastoral Education and the College of Chaplains, Atlanta, groups which in 1966 and 1972 honored Dr. Dobbins with Distinguished Service Awards, are developments of this aspect of pastoral care.) On the other hand it leads to individual (as well as group) care for those who are divorced, single, married, sick, emotionally disturbed, in need of spiritual guidance, faced with problem children and problem parents, unable to cope with problems of life. (Marital and Family Counseling is perhaps the most widely known aspect of this portion of pastoral care.)

Dr. Dobbins is generally recognized for his work in church administration. He is less widely recognized for his innovative work in pastoral care, which he regarded as a branch of administration. Dr. Oates notes that Dr. Dobbins gave him credit for initiating the pastoral care movement in seminary education. Actually, he says, it was Dr. Dobbins who, beginning in 1937, initiated the concept.

> He started this work. He equipped me to carry it to fruition, . . . but if it had not been for his sponsorship of me and his leadership in the organization of the work, I would never have made it. [Together] we explored the relationship between religion and medicine, psychotherapy and the Christian faith, and a Christian apologetic in the fact of the clinical discoveries of psychoanalysis. This was uncharted territory. I wanted to find teachers who had worked all these things out and had the answers. Dr. Dobbins rightly told me that there were none. We would have to work it out on our own (*Great Teachers*, 1965).

Out of book study, work in the churches, and practical experience at the Louisville City Hospital, Central State Hospital, Ormsby Village Treatment Center, and Norton Psychiatric Clinic, Dr. Dobbins' students developed a new—yet old—field of study, pastoral care.

To Dr. Dobbins, pastoral care—the attempt "to make all of life Christian"—was a concept that unified the fields of church administration and religious education. In *Zest for Living*, which presents the clearest statement of his point of view, he wrote, "Pastoral care is not a separate and optional ministry but an attitude and function relating to and renewing all other responsibilities." In that it recognizes that personality is complex and that truth is holistic, not scattered and fragmentary, it

> brings to worship a sense of involvement with God and fellow Christians, the inspiration and resolution to make all of life more Christlike. It brings to preach-

ing a freshness and power that enables the proclaimer to view the congregation as individuals searching for solutions, solutions which can best be found as God in Christ through the Holy Spirit speaks to their needs and sends them out on a mission of high adventure. It brings to teaching a person-mindedness that saves the teacher from teaching "lessons" and gives him the lift that comes from teaching persons. It brings compassion to interpersonal relations when every contact is viewed as a potential transaction with an infinitely precious human being for whom Christ died. It brings to a person's outlook on life the undefeatable optimism that while skirmishes may be lost the battle for and with Christ eventually will be won. This Christlike person-mindedness will sustain enthusiasm for evangelism in spite of all obstacles and odds.

Thus pastoral care is the responsibility of every minister. Indeed, as Dr. Oates states, "Ministry to individuals, families, and small groups in times of crisis and intense personal need is the responsibility of every Christian" (*Encyclopedia of Southern Baptists*, 1958, II, 1073). It is a concept that applies to every deacon, Sunday School teacher, educational and music director, member of the WMU or Brotherhood. "The church itself," says Dr. Oates, "is a prayerful fellowship of concern, a community of pastoral care." Worship, preaching, teaching, interpersonal relations, attitude toward life—each requires "Christlike person-mindedness," an attitude which seeks to meet the spiritual needs of each individual, regardless of his or her condition. The problem of this type of ministry is not that it is too complex but that it requires a knowledge of the best in every field.

What is a minister? To Dr. Dobbins, a minister is a preacher, but he is more than a preacher. He is a teacher, but he is more than a teacher. He is a preacher-teacher-administrator-counselor; whether ordained or a layman, he is a shepherd, a pastor who, giving his best, goes out into the highways and byways to seek and to save the lost. The concept is awesome, for it requires unqualified dedication, continuous service, rigorous training, administratively and otherwise, the utmost in compassion, and wholehearted, sacrificial love of God and man. These are complex requirements, but in the service of God who would do less than his best?

6
Administrator

Vividly I recall the meeting of the Executive Committee of the Convention in 1933 [1931] at Nashville. Report after report of the Convention's boards and agencies indicated practical bankruptcy. At length Dr. L. R. Scarborough, president of Southwestern Seminary, arose and choking with emotion said in effect, "Brethren, we are through at Southwestern. For two years we haven't paid faculty salaries. We have nothing with which to meet expenses. Our percentage of the allocation will not see us through another year. Here is my resignation and I turn over to you the seminary property. You'll have to sell it to pay our debts and Southwestern will go out of existence."

There was a stunned silence. We sat in tears. Then Dr. Sampey arose, drummed with his fingers on the table in characteristic fashion, and said in effect, "I may lose my job for what I am about to say. Southern Seminary has some income from endowment on which we can live. I move that Southern Seminary's apportionment be cut and the difference be given to Southwestern" (*Great Teachers*, 1965).

The magnificence of Dr. Sampey's proposal may be indicated by recalling that in 1931 the United States was in the midst of the worst depression the country had faced since 1893. In three years, from 1929 through 1931, gifts from Southern Baptists to Convention causes decreased from $2,227,290 to $1,682,534, almost 25 percent. During this period, Southern's income from the Convention decreased $85,000. The loss of funds did not bankrupt the Seminary, but in 1931 Southern was in almost as critical a position financially as was Southwestern. In 1925-26 Southern had conducted a campaign, largely in Florida, to secure funds to pay for its new campus. The campaign had succeeded, but with the coming of the depression the pledges had become worthless, leaving an unpaid debt (in 1931) of $695,000. By 1932, including unpaid interest, Southern was more than $150,000 behind in payments. Moreover, in 1930-31, two of the banks in which the

Seminary had deposited its funds had gone into receivership, largely tying up the Seminary's operating and student aid funds. As a result, although the Seminary was not bankrupt, in 1931 it was close to the edge.

Thus Dr. Sampey's proposal that Southern Seminary's allotment from the Cooperative Program be cut was considerably more than a gesture. It was something that *had to be done.* Even if it resulted in hardship for Southern, Southwestern could not be allowed to close. The move achieved its purpose. It gave Southwestern "a new lease on life," but it left problems. It might have reduced Southern's income as much as $15,000 or 5 percent of its annual income, depending upon the percentage of Cooperative Program funds allotted to Southern in 1932. Fortunately this did not happen. Instead, although its income continued to decrease, in 1932 Southern's Cooperative Program percentage remained unchanged. By using methods of strict economy Southern managed to stay within its budget.

Dr. Sampey was a generous man, but, as he himself recognized, he was not an administrator. Seeking someone with practical experience, he asked Dr. Dobbins to assume the position of Seminary Treasurer—without salary. Dr. Dobbins would be expected to continue his teaching, of course. No money was available to hire someone to teach his courses. Dr. Dobbins was a logical choice, for not only did he have administrative background but also since 1928 unofficially he had assisted Dr. Sampey in financial affairs. At first Dr. Dobbins was reluctant to accept the assignment. He did not particularly object to working without salary. Since 1929 he had been "pastor without emolument" at Buechel (Park) Baptist Church, a church that needed help. Serving without pay was not particularly unusual for a seminary professor. His objection rather was that acceptance of the position as treasurer would take him away from his teaching and writing and possibly lead to faculty jealousy. (And it did.) Yet the Seminary needed his help. And apparently there was no one else who could (or would) assume the responsibility. Actually, as had been true so many times in his life, Dr. Dobbins had little choice. His life was not his own but Christ's. He was called to serve. In May 1933, in addition to his responsibilities as teacher, preacher, and author (lesson writer for *Sunday School Young People and Adults* and the *Baptist Adult Union Quarterly,* which he founded), Dr. Dobbins became treasurer of Southern Seminary, a position which he retained for nine years. In May 1934, he became assistant financial agent as well.

As treasurer and financial agent Dr. Dobbins faced a difficult, even desperate situation. Southern could not raise tuition. The Seminary charged no tuition. The Seminary could expect no additional money from the Convention. Except for Mission Board campaigns, the Convention refused to permit special fund-raising drives. The Cooperative Program allotment might be increased, and was (from 3⅓ to 4⅕ percent), but receipts did not return to their 1928 level until 1935. Little help could be expected from the Sunday School Board, the agency which had given so generously to Southern and other Convention causes in the past. With a three-year reduction in income of almost 20 percent, the Board was in no condition to make contributions. There was only one possible additional source of funds, voluntary contributions from the newly organized "Hundred Thousand Club," a club that proposed that Southern Baptists pay the debts of Convention agencies by giving a dollar a month "over and above" their regular gifts (Remember?). With receipts from the Hundred Thousand Club, in December 1934, Southern was able to cancel three $1,000 notes. The debt that remained, for the time, was enormous, but this at least began the repayment. By 1944, through its "widows' mites," the Club's contributions of more than $500,000 largely enabled Southern to pay its debts.

But 1944 was not 1933. In 1933, for student aid, salaries, library expenses, upkeep of grounds and buildings, and supplies and expenses, Southern had an income of $306,000. How does one operate a virtually insolvent institution? When asked this question, Dr. Dobbins answered reminiscently, with a smile, "By cutting expenses to the bone, by reducing faculty and other salaries to a bare minimum." In 1932 three administrative positions were eliminated and faculty salaries were cut 30 percent. As a result Dr. Dobbins unofficially also became publicity director and alumni secretary for the Seminary. In 1933 he had the unpleasant task of telling his colleagues that the Seminary might be unable to pay more than half their salaries, a cut of 50 rather than 30 percent. The additional reduction was not necessary, but it might have been required—and worse. There was a real possibility that Southern might be forced to close.

"I'll never forget the meeting in Dr. Sampey's office with the committee from the Fidelity and Columbia Trust Company" (the holder of the Seminary notes), Dr. Dobbins told Dr. Dillard in 1978.

"We've got to have some settlement," insisted one of the committee members. "The bank examiner is after us and we can't continue with nonpayment even with interest."

Then another of the bank members said, looking at Dr. Sampey, "You are a scholar. What does the word 'mortgage' mean?"

Dr. Sampey turned pale. Sweat came out on his face. "You wouldn't foreclose?" he asked. "You know what that would mean. What alternative do we have?"

The spokesman for the bank replied, "We don't want the Seminary property. You've already built on it. It would certainly be one of the most unpopular things we could do to foreclose. But your downtown property [the old Seminary campus] is unencumbered. If you will sign it over to us, we will count that as a down payment and extend your mortgage."

I shook my head. "How much would be the estimate?" I asked.

"$200,000."

"Oh, my soul," I said. "That's a million dollar property right in the heart of downtown Louisville."

"Well, that's the highest we can go. You think it over. We'll give you sixty days" (Dillard Tape, 1978; *The Alabama Baptist*, Dec. 12, 1974).

August through September, then foreclosure. The property on Broadway would be lost. Then a three months' extension of time was granted. During this period Dr. Dobbins asked Mr. W. L. Lyons, a broker, to help the Seminary refinance its loan. In December he received a telegram from New York: "City National Bank [Mutual Benefit Life Insurance Company] is taking over the full amount of your mortgage and is putting the money to your credit." On February 1, 1935, through Mr. Lyons' efforts, the full amount of Southern's indebtedness of $590,000 was refinanced at 5 percent, a reduction of 1 percent interest. "It was a happy moment," Dr. Dobbins recalled, "when I stood at the window of the local bank and received the cancelled notes." In 1937 the Louisville bank offered to renew the loan at 4½ percent interest, an offer, Dr. Dobbins stated,

which was promptly met by the insurance company at 4 per cent. The bank tried again [in 1938], offering to meet the insurance company's 4 per cent interest rate, whereupon the insurance company lowered its rate to 3½ per cent on condition that the loan remain with their company until fully paid (*Baptist History and Heritage*, July 1970).

By 1942, when Dr. Ellis Fuller, Southern's sixth president, was inaugurated, all but $180,000 of the debt had been paid. It is estimated that the refinancings of the Seminary loan, including income received from the downtown property, saved the Seminary at least $300,000 from 1935-1942. The story is told not simply to praise Dr. Dobbins, for clearly he was not wholly responsible for the series of events. Dr. Sampey, W. L. Lyons, W. J. Wilder, Charles Burts, George Norton, V. V. Cooke, and others, also were responsible for retaining possession of the Seminary's downtown property, until recently the most valuable tangible possession the Seminary owned. Under the leadership of God, Dr. Dobbins was simply the right man at the right place.

And at the right time, a time of desperation, of greed, and nobility, a time of courage and of willingness to serve. "I remember the depression," Dr. Dobbins wrote in 1974. He did, distinctly. Temporarily unable to pay the $100 a month due on his own mortgage, he also was threatened with foreclosure by the local bank. However, since the deed to the house was in his wife's name, he was not forced to vacate. The car, which kept running, lasted for nine years. Mr. Potts, the grocer, advanced credit for months, and somehow, through money he earned from teaching, lecturing, preaching, and writing articles and books (7 of which he wrote from 1930 to 1938), he managed to support and educate his family. Yes, Dr. Dobbins recalled the depression distinctly. It was a frightening experience.

With 12,000,000 workers seeking employment, jobs were scarce. At the Seminary, students lacked money even to buy food. Hearing of a student family in trouble, Dr. Dobbins wrote, he

> went to their apartment [in Judson Hall] to see about it. A tear-stained mother came to the door when I knocked. I inquired for her husband. "He's away looking for work," she replied. "Have you and the children anything to eat?" Reluctantly she opened the door, went to the kitchen table, and pointed to a small basket of specked apples. "That's all we've had for the past three days." I hurried back to the office and managed to get a small check to tide the family over (*The Alabama Baptist,* Dec. 12, 1974; "Founders Day Address," Southern Seminary, Sept. 15, 1966).

In 1933 Seminary enrollment dropped to 343, the lowest point since 1920. Something had to be done—and quickly. Since the Seminary itself was impoverished, money for student aid was limited, but food, which farmers were unable to market, was available. With the help of farmers and Christian businessmen and pastors from the Louisville area, Dr. Dobbins set up a commissary in the basement of Rice Hall. A small cannery was established and a quantity of canned goods stored for the winter. Food vouchers were issued (an early food stamp program). Letters were sent to selected lay people throughout the Convention: "Adopt a student. Send $15.00 and feed a student a month" (*Western Recorder,* June 28, 1934). Checks began to arrive. Southern Baptists did not have much money, but they had generous hearts. Fifty cents a day, of course, did not provide lavish meals, but no one went hungry. And none of the students had to leave the Seminary for lack of food.

As treasurer of Southern, Dr. Dobbins applied the principles of administration which he advocated in his classes and in his writing. The effective administrator, he wrote in *Baptist Churches in Action* (1929), recognizes three functions of management: (1) To discover the needs to be met. In 1933 the needs of the Seminary were obvious, to keep the Seminary open and to support its students. (2) To discover the resources of the church (the Seminary). Southern's resources were people, pastors, farmers, businessmen who loved and wanted to assist the Seminary provided they were asked to help. And (3) To secure competent leadership. To George Norton, George Stoll, J. H. Anderson, Charles Gheens, and other influential men he sent out appeals for help. They responded generously, giving both money and time, in trustee meetings, in furnishing student training facilities, and in contacting other friends of the Seminary. From the state alumni presidents, he secured names of selected individuals who might be persuaded to include the Seminary in their wills. Then, appealing to the alumni, he attempted to increase the Seminary's endowment.

Earlier, in 1932, Dr. Dobbins had proposed that the alumni undertake to raise $100,000 to endow a Chair of Old Testament Interpretation in honor of Dr. Sampey ("Tiglath"), who would be seventy in 1933. The proposal was accepted enthusiastically, but depression slowed the gathering of funds. By 1937, Dr. Sampey's fiftieth year of association with the Seminary, receipts totaled $55,000, an increase of $11,000 a year. In 1936, acting on behalf of the alumni, Dr. Dobbins sought to complete the campaign. Records with a message from Dr. Sampey were sent to the churches where his former students were pastors. So determined was Dr. Dobbins to raise money for the Sampey Chair, it was said, that he sometimes "billed" a church for more than it had anticipated paying for his preaching, with the entire sum designated for the Chair. (Certainly he used this method in 1946 when he sought to raise money for the Alumni Memorial Chapel.) In December 1937, to save Dr. Sampey embarrassment, the trustees of the Seminary forbad any further attempts to raise funds. Abiding strictly by the letter of the trustees' decision, nevertheless Dr. Dobbins continued his efforts. He made no further appeals to the alumni. Instead he published a general letter. "We are within $5,000 of the goal," he wrote.

> Doctor Sampey requested the Board of Trustees to forbid the writer making any further direct appeals for the Endowment of the Chair after December 31, 1937. But there is no restraint on his making known the facts; and some of us who have had our hearts so deeply set on the completion of the Endowment in full by the meeting of the Convention [in Richmond] in May are praying in faith and in confidence that the remaining $5,000 will appear before this date (*Western Recorder,* March 3, 1938).

And in May, with the help of a gift of $10,000 from J. H. Anderson, the Sampey Chair was endowed! The total amounted to $105,000.

In 1942, with the inauguration of Dr. Ellis Fuller as the sixth president of the Seminary, Dr. Dobbins was permitted to resign his position as treasurer. He was not allowed to discontinue his financial activities, however, for he was asked to continue his fund-raising responsibilities by the new president. First, to obtain funds for student aid. During 1941-47, and perhaps later, Dr. Dobbins made arrangements for Lynn Elder, J. P. Colvin, Fred Laughon, and other students to visit the churches to show a film designed to secure pledges for student aid. By 1947 the Seminary was enabled to increase its student aid (including loans) from $41,000 to $52,000, or approximately 20 percent. Second, to obtain funds for the Alumni Chapel, a building which had been included in the plans for the new campus but which, because of the depression, had not been built. Working with the alumni, Dr. Dobbins organized a fund-raising campaign, setting goals: Alabama, $20,600, Arkansas, $6,000, District of Columbia, $2,000, Florida, $14,900, Georgia, $23,600, Illinois, $4,600, Indiana, $7,500 . . . for a total of $273,000. With the help of C. C. Warren, Bruce H. Price, and many other alumni, the fund was completed. In March 1950, the Alumni Memorial Chapel (perhaps better called "Fuller Chapel") was dedicated. Tragically, on October 28, 1950, Dr. Fuller, the guiding spirit behind the building of the Chapel, died. The Chapel is one of his memorials.

The picture presented above of Dr. Dobbins as an administrator, a practical "Vice President for Business Affairs," may seem contradictory to those who regard Dr. Dobbins primarily as an academician. Surely he was too theoretically minded, too sweet tempered, too Christian to be a successful businessman. No! for although the characterization, I think, is accurate (Dr. Dobbins was interested in ideas, he was gentle and compassionate in his nature, and he tried to live by Christian principles), the implication that business and Christianity are ill at ease in each other's presence Dr. Dobbins denied vigorously. The topic deserves some emphasis, for the concept of the relationship of business to Christianity was close to Dr. Dobbins' heart. In his early writings he maintained that the church is a business—Christ's business, nevertheless a business. This relationship he examined carefully in seven of the books which he published between 1923 and 1976. In his last (unpublished) manuscript (1976-77), the title, "The Mutuality of Business and Religion," indicates his continued interest in the subject.

To Dr. Dobbins, business and religion were not identical. Both he regarded, however, as parts of a whole. (Truth is not composed of scattered parts.) Business is concerned with life fulfillment, morality, management and ministry, goals, motivations, community involvement, and planning. With the addition of Christ as Savior and Master, Christianity seeks similar ends. Central in both fields, according to Wilbert E. Moore, *The Professionals* (1970), George T. Lockland, *Grow or Die* (1973), John B. Miner, *The Management Process* (1973), and other writers, is recognition of the value of the individual (Manuscript, 1976-77). As an effective administrator, a businessman begins by determining human needs, both those of his customers and of his employees, responds to these needs by developing adequate resources, and uses these resources efficiently by obtaining leadership responses. So similarly does an effective editor, educator, seminary administrator, lawyer, Sunday School teacher, and minister.

In a sense, Dr. Dobbins' view that there is a relationship between business and religion was the concept that Arthur Flake had preached in 1919. Dr. Dobbins, as did Dr. Flake, questioned the view that secular and Christian activities are "somehow different." Dr. Flake was no less a businessman as a Sunday School administrator than he had been as a dry goods merchant before he joined the staff of the Sunday School Board. Dr. Dobbins did not regard himself as a businessman (treasurer) six days a week and as a minister on Sunday. His two activities were mutually related and actually one. Compartmentalization, of course, is possible. A minister may regard his occupation, in contradistinction to that of a layman, as a particular God-chosen calling. A businessman may object,

> I live in a world of keen competition and inescapable demands. Under these pressures I couldn't survive and also live up to the requirements of strict Christian ethics. I might make it if my competitors and stockholders would also agree, but they won't. I keep my business ethics and practices in one compartment and my Christian faith and ideals in another. I try not to let them conflict too sharply, but I have to compromise at times or lose my job. If I get fired and lose my income, my church would lose my support—and that wouldn't be good, would it? And so I separate the two areas of my life, keeping alive as a businessman and conscience-free as a church member (Ms., 1976-77).

To Dr. Dobbins, neither of the views presented above was biblical, for, according to the Bible, not only were many of the early ministers businessmen but as businessmen they also were ministers. Abraham, Isaac, Jacob, David, Moses, and many of the other great characters of the Old Testament had secular occupations. Jesus himself instructed the twelve, and later the seventy, in business methods. Paul was cautious and business minded in handling the collections entrusted to him for delivery to the Christians in Jerusalem. Biblically no conflict exists between business and religion. Both are or at least may be Christian. Conflict arises when an individual, minister or layman, fails to permit Christ to determine his goals. As a follower of Christ, one's calling is not to be a minister or a layman but to be a Christian.

As an administrator-minister, Dr. Dobbins was deeply concerned with the tendency among Southern Baptists to separate the clergy from the laity and the laity from the clergy. In a denomination which believes in the "priesthood of believers," he maintained, this trend should be avoided as much as possible. Ordination does not make one a minister. Whether one is a minister or a layman, one's calling is to witness for Christ. Is there, then, no difference between the calls to witness experienced by both minister and layman? This question Dr. Dobbins answered with an emphatic yes! The call to full-time Christian ministry is unique. It is unique because

> (1) It represents a vocation which deals primarily with the human spirit; (2) it seeks through human agency to link man with God; and (3) it conserves all other values (Summarized from *Building Better Churches*, 1947).

Nevertheless, he pointed out,

> there is nothing which the pastor does (unless it be of a civil or contractual nature) which could not be delegated by him or the church to an unordained member. Thus a layman, authorized by his church, can preach, teach, pray, administer the ordinances, supervise the organizations, visit the sick, bury the dead, serve on councils and committees, or render any other service whatever. . . . There is little New Testament justification for a sharp distinction between the responsibility of the pastor as being "spiritual" and that of the deacon [the layman] as being "material" *(Encyclopedia of Southern Baptists,* 1958, I, 278).

> A church, at its best, is a spiritual democracy. Its government is of the people, by the people, for the people. In a democratic church, the rulers are the ruled. Leadership is necessary, but the leaders are selected by the people and are amenable to them *(The Churchbook,* 1951).

Similar statements appear in *The Efficient Church* (1923), *Baptist Churches in Action* (1929), and *Can a Religious Democracy Survive?* (1941).

A minister, Dr. Dobbins believed, is not a hired man, nor is he a boss. Rather he is "God's divinely appointed pastor of the flock, overseer of the work of the church, leader of the people, undershepherd of Christ, servant of all" *(Baptist Churches in Action).* Through the guidance of the Holy Spirit, in the name of Christ, he is to serve, enlist, inspire, and guide *people,* his flock. Embodied in this one word, *people,* people who need, will respond to and serve Christ, is to be found the minister's chief function.

> The church's message must be incarnated in men and women who translate the language of scripture into the language of life. The supreme goal of a church is, therefore, the growing of Christian character *(Working Together in a Spiritual Democracy,* 1935). . . . Here, then, is the starting point in disciple winning, a principle of method which, if violated, makes all else void. We who would win others to be Christ's disciples must test all our methods by the question: *Does it respect personality? (Evangelism According to Christ,* 1949). . . . When John A. Broadus was asked, "What are the essentials of an effective sermon?" he replied, "First, a sympathetic, responsive congregation; second, a sympathetic, responsive congregation; third, a sympathetic, responsive congregation" *(Good News to Change Lives,* 1976).

Since in his writing, teaching, and preaching, Dr. Dobbins maintained that the church, Christ's method of spreading the gospel, is people-centered, it is not surprising that he was widely respected as an able leader and administrator. At Southern, from 1933 to 1950, as treasurer, publicity director, director of the pastor's conference, development officer, alumni secretary, supervisor of buildings and grounds (during the 1937 flood), and, of course, professor of religious education and church administration, he served in more different positions than anyone else had filled in the history of the Seminary. In the community he served as supply pastor at Buechel, Bagdad, Cedar Creek, Broadway, Eastern Parkway, Temple, and Bardstown Road. On the denominational level he served as chairman of the committee on church organizations, conducted at least 50 clinics and conferences, and published 13 books (and over 2,400 reviews and articles).

Given an assignment, Dr. Dobbins served efficiently and ably. Why was he so successful as a leader? Humanly speaking, I think, largely because he recognized the importance of the individual in decision-making. Dr. Findley Edge touches on this idea when he says that as a beginning teacher at Southern in 1944 he hoped that Dr. Dobbins, as senior professor, would furnish him guidance in teaching in the form of old notes and outlines. This Dr. Dobbins refused to do, saying instead, "Brother Edge, this is *your* 'little red wagon.' I want *you* to pull it." Initially Dr. Edge reacted with frustration. Then, he says, he recognized that "Dr. Dobbins knew that I was a man and he expected me to act like one. He knew I had potential and he gave me the freedom to develop it" *(Review and Expositor,* July 1978).

Dr. Wayne Oates, to whom Dr. Dobbins also turned over his courses while he went on to other fields, calls Dr. Dobbins "a motivator of individual initiative. . . . He assumed that I could do anything that any student could, that I *wanted* to learn and grow. He enabled me to believe this myself" *(Great Teachers,* 1965).

Similar statements are made by virtually everyone with whom Dr. Dobbins was associated. He expected his students, laymen, fellow professors, yes, and his family as well, to act responsibly. Through study, first, of things (of books), then, of practical experience (with people), he expected his associates to make their own decisions or, colloquially stated, to "stand on their own two feet."

To Dr. Dobbins, people, not things, were important. Asked if he didn't get tired of teaching the same things year after year, his reply was, "No, for I do not teach things. I teach persons—and they are fascinatingly different, session after session" *(Zest for Living*, 1977). Identifying themselves with this point of view, people responded and willingly followed his direction.

As a result, in 1950, with the untimely death of Dr. Ellis Fuller, Southern's board of trustees turned to Dr. Dobbins for leadership. In 1933, Dr. Dobbins had been a logical choice as treasurer of the Seminary. Seventeen years later, because he understood and motivated people, he was a logical choice as interim or acting president, a position which he held from November 24, 1950 to September 14, 1951 (9½ months). Briefly Dr. Dobbins and Dr. Jesse B. Weatherspoon served as co-interim presidents. Dr. Weatherspoon, however, asked that he be excused from duty. As president, as an experienced administrator and senior member of the faculty, Dr. Dobbins was beloved and respected by almost all who knew him. The phrase "almost all" has been added with some hesitation, for it points to the beginning of a crisis that developed to the critical point seven years later.

In 1943, seeking to meet the needs of the churches, Dr. Ellis Fuller had inaugurated a school of music at Southern. Since the addition of this school apparently involved changes in the educational objectives of the Seminary, disapproval was expressed by a number of the members of the theological faculty, who also objected to the support which the administration gave to courses in church administration, religious education, pastoral care, children's work, and the other subjects which constitute the practical field. "Except for some of the trustees," said Dr. Dobbins, "to Dr. Fuller belongs more credit than anyone else for the school of education which was established in 1954" (Combs Tape, March 3, 1977). Dr. Fuller and, later, Dr. Duke McCall sought to make Southern a school which would be both scholarly and practical—to continue the tradition of presidents Sampey and Mullins. At issue was the question of the nature of ministerial education. Should Southern follow the pattern of a divinity school in its curriculum or should it train its students for multiple ministries? Other issues were involved. However, so far as Dr. Dobbins was concerned, the controversy was an educational one—in part a continuation of the faculty objection of the 1920s. In 1958-59, the question of whether Southern should remain solely or partially within the "body of divinity" was resolved—at least immediately—with the resignation/dismissal of thirteen professors.

In 1950-51, however, no unshakable commitments had been made.

It is to Dr. Dobbins' credit that, although he was a member of the Music and Education group, he was able to help keep the controversy under control. Referring to the members of the opposing group, Dr. Dobbins remarked in 1978,

I give them credit for being honest and earnest—they were not seeking power. They were seeking to maintain what they thought was the ideal future of the Seminary, that it be a Theological Seminary—and to bring in Religious Education and Music students was unheard of. But that's not what the churches wanted, and they wouldn't have supported the Seminary on that basis (Dillard Tape, 1978).

During his term as interim president, Dr. Dobbins faced a second crisis which deserves mention. In September 1951, blacks (American blacks) were admitted to classes at Southern on an equal basis with whites. The action is worth noting, for the Supreme Court's decision regarding desegregation was not issued until 1954, three years later. Since 1940, members of the faculty had taught Negro students privately in their offices and homes. At the time it was against Kentucky law for blacks and whites to be taught in the same classroom. Vexed by the restriction, Southern students petitioned the trustees to permit equal admission to qualified students regardless of their race. At first the request was rejected. In 1950, supported by a poll of student opinion, the students again requested the trustees to permit equal admission. As might be expected, it was Dr. Dobbins who suggested that the poll be taken. Of 754 students who expressed their opinion, 714 indicated approval, 27 no opinion, and 13 disapproval. In March 1950, with the unanimous approval of the faculty, the trustees voted to grant qualified Negroes unrestricted admission "to classes, library, and all academic rights and privileges" beginning with the 1951-52 session. As acting president, it was Dr. Dobbins' responsibility to respond to criticism, which was not wholly favorable, and to implement the trustees' decision by obtaining Convention support.

To determine the reaction of Southern's constituency to the admission of blacks, following the practice he taught in his classes, Dr. Dobbins "took a census." Of the 62 state secretaries, presidents of colleges, and denominational leaders who responded to his poll, 39 approved the admission of blacks, 5 expressed mixed feelings, and 18 voiced disapproval. Clearly, Southern's students were less conservative than their denominational leaders. However, the denominational leaders were more in agreement with the thinking of the Convention as a whole, for, although in 1954 the Convention voted to support the Supreme Court's decision concerning segregation, the vote was by no means unanimous. In 1950, with Southern Baptist response undetermined, the action of the trustees took considerable courage.

Personally, Dr. Dobbins regarded the admission of blacks to Southern with unqualified approval. Applied to a Southerner born in 1886, this statement is more unusual than at first might appear. In 1905, as editor of *The Saturday Evening Eye,* Gaines Dobbins referred to Negroes as "barbaric humans with no ideals, no conception of anything at all that makes up the life of those who stand high in the great plan of things." In 1951, in a release sent to the Baptist denominational press, Dr. Dobbins expressed quite a different point of view. "When Baptists [Christians] confront a need," he wrote, "the question is not, 'What is expedient and popular?' but 'What would Christ have us do?' " *(The Tie,* April 1951). Seventeen years later, at Selma and Birmingham, he was leading conferences designed to improve race relations in Alabama. A large portion of Southern history is summed up in the two quotations given above. The change of attitude, of course, was not Dr. Dobbins' alone. The South changed—not completely but significantly, and both as leader and follower Dr. Dobbins changed also. Personally and individually, believing in the infinite value of everyone, regardless of heredity, as a Christian he sought to act as Christ would have him act.

In his *History of Southern Baptist Theological Seminary* (1959), Dr. William A. Mueller ably summarizes the tangible results of Dr. Dobbins' activities as president. During Dr. Dobbins' term of office, writes Dr. Mueller,

> Extensive remodeling and enlarging of the library took place, the old chapel being transformed into a large reading room. A child care program was set up for the benefit of married students, and the term system was replaced by the semester system. In conjunction with other Southern Baptist seminaries, Dr. Dobbins helped establish an extension department for less educated ministers. Steps were also taken to raise standards for admission to graduate study in the Seminary.

There is little more that needs to be written of Dr. Dobbins' term as interim president, for actually, although the period of his presidency was significant, to Dr. Dobbins more significant than his term as president was his election in 1953 to the position of dean of the School of Religious Education, under the leadership of Dr. Duke K. McCall, the seventh president of the Seminary.

Dr. Dobbins was *delighted* at the nomination and election of Dr. McCall as president. He (Dr. Dobbins) might have been president of Blue Mountain College (1925), of Southeastern (1951), of Southern (1951). Instead, he asked that he not be considered for the positions. Immediately after he was elected interim president, he stated, "I would not swap my teaching for any position in the world" *(Courier-Journal,* Nov. 25, 1950). Nor as acting president did he give up his teaching duties. Perhaps for once he was inconsistent in his attitude. Theoretically he should have enjoyed administrative responsibilities. Actually his major interest lay in dealing with people. Perhaps the two attitudes can be combined: Dr. Dobbins enjoyed administrative duties so long as they dealt with people.

In *Building Better Churches* (1947), Dr. Dobbins described the ideal pastor (teacher) as being "person-minded." This type of minister, he said,

> will face every aspect of his task and every activity of his church with the question: *What personality values are being created and conserved?* This question will give guidance to his study, his preaching, his teaching, his pastoral visiting, his supervision, his work of administration, his counseling, his praying. "Machinery" will lose its sanctity except as means to sacred ends, and these ends are *persons*—the Glory of God and human well-being.

The minister whom Dr. Dobbins described might well be regarded as a portrait of Dr. Dobbins himself. Person-mindedness was the heart of his ministry. Dr. McCall's coming made it possible for him to return to his first love, people—students, those with whom he could enjoy the stimulation and enlargement that comes from disseminating ideas of God and Christ.

People. Can people be taught to teach and to operate a church efficiently? Dr. McCall, and before Dr. McCall, Dr. Mullins, Dr. Sampey, Dr. Fuller, the four great presidents of Southern under whom Dr. Dobbins served, believed in the principle of a people's church as a major Baptist distinctive. Oh, if only this concept could be gotten across to the ministerial students, now more than 1,000, who thronged Southern's campus each year! True, under God the church is a theocracy. Humanly regarded, however, the church is a democracy, a community of lay persons who are guided by a pastor under the leadership of Christ. Is it possible for *demos*, the people, to rule effectively? To this question the Baptist answer (the answer of the Reformation) is a resounding yes! "God alone is Lord of the conscience . . . the sole authority for faith and practice among Baptists is the Scriptures of the Old and New Testaments" *(Baptist Faith and Message,* 1925, 1963).

Acceptance of this view places responsibility on the individual, the lay person, to assume a place of leadership. Yet this is impossible, humanly speaking, unless the lay person understands the Bible. This, then, is the function of religious education: "To develop soul-winning personal workers in the ranks of the laity who will make possible the apostolic ideal of adding unto the church day by day those that are saved" ("Inaugural Address," 1920). To fulfill this purpose pastors must be trained to understand their place as leaders of leaders, specialists must be provided to help the pastors of the 1,200 Southern Baptist churches which (in 1954) had congregations of more than 1,000 members, and church members (deacons, Sunday School teachers, WMU workers, . . . lay people) must be taught to "share with Christ and with one another in the saving of lost persons who will then be the saving salt in a decaying society" *(The Church at Worship,* 1962).

Could this be done? Can lay people be taught to witness effectively for Christ? To Dr. Dobbins, the enthusiastic response of *thousands* of those whom he had taught at Ridgecrest Baptist Assembly, in the churches, through the lesson quarterlies, and at Southern proved unquestionably that lay persons could be taught to become effective witnesses. From 1920 to 1944 he had operated a "one-man School of Religious Education"; this approach no longer was adequate. (Actually, at Southern, Dr. Byron DeMent taught a course in Religious Education as early as 1906.) Before 1938, when the Seminary permitted matriculation of nonordained students, there were relatively few large Baptist churches. During the "Decade of Correlation and Specialization" (1940-50), however, the situation changed. To Dr. Dobbins' office yearly there came 500 requests for specialists who could aid churches with their problems. With the change in the nature of the WMU Training School to a "School of Missions and Social Work" in 1952, the need for additional courses in Religious Education at Southern became acute. For an estimated increase of 100-150 students, three additional instructors would be required. What an opportunity—within ten years to meet the educational and administrative needs of more than 1,000,000 Baptists! Surely, then, establishment of Southern's School of Religious Education provided greater opportunity than fulfilling the duties of a president.

In March 1953, Dr. Dobbins became the first dean of Southern's School of Religious Education, a school for which Dr. Fuller had planned and Dr. McCall made possible. In the fall of 1954, the first year of the School of Religious Education's operation, a department staffed by one professor in 1920 required six in 1954. Two courses in 1920 became 38 in 1954. What were Dr. Dobbins' most outstanding accomplishments as dean of the School of Religious Education? Three should be mentioned: First, the selection of his staff: Findley Edge, Denton Coker, Sabin Landry, Ernest Loessner, Pauline Hargis, and (later) Robert Proctor. "Nothing I have ever done," Dr. Dobbins remarked in 1970, "has been quite so gratifying as the way these 'lads' have made good" (Rawls Videotape, 1970). It is to Dr. Dobbins' credit that the faculty of the RE School included an instructor named Ernest Loessner, the only instructor without a college degree ever elected to the faculty at Southern. In 1970, eighteen years later, having earned his doctor's degree, Dr. Loessner became the third dean of the School. Second, the acceptance of the School of Religious Education as an integral part of the Seminary (of equal status with the School of Theology). And third, the establishment of a curriculum which was equal or superior to any other religious education program in the country.

What is a minister of religious education? After one to three or more years of study, wrote Dr. Dobbins, a graduate of the School of Religious Education, a minister of education, should be prepared:

1. To assist in discovering and enlisting teachers, officers and leaders for the Sunday School and Training Union.

2. To have general oversight of the program of leadership training for the teachers, officers, and leaders.

3. To give general direction and inspiration to plans for promotion and enlargement.

4. To give guidance to the worker's conference, the weekly officers and teachers' meeting, the monthly planning meeting of the Training Union.

5. To set up and encourage a program of continuous visitation of absentees and prospective members.

6. To have general oversight of the records and their constructive use.

7. To study the needs of Sunday School, Training Union, W.M.U. in the matter of literature and "helps" and to order economically the best available materials.

8. To assist in the planning of departmental and assembly programs and programs for special occasions.

9. To plan well in advance for the success of the Daily Vacation Bible School.

10. To utilize all these resources for evangelism and the upbuilding of the church.

11. To correlate all the educational activities so as to give them greater unity.

12. To keep in close touch with the pastor so that the plans for the church as a whole and the plans for the organizations of the church shall be coordinated.

The quotation is from a letter written by Dr. Dobbins to Dr. W. A. Sullivan, pastor of the First Baptist Church, Natchez, October 10, 1946. Similar lists appear in *The Churchbook* (1951) and *A Ministering Church* (1960). After rereading his letter, Dr. Dobbins concluded wryly, "Perhaps I have suggested too many responsibilities. Yet they must be fulfilled; the educational director will do whatever he or she can do personally and then find and enlist capable persons to do the rest. I wish we had fifty such qualified persons available right now to meet the demands."

Dr. Dobbins made little distinction between a minister of education and a pastor. The minister is the church's chief of staff. The minister of education is his chief assistant. Both are servants of God. It was Dr. Dobbins' privilege to teach God's servants at Southern for 36 years. The School of Religious Education is his monument—a living memorial. To be dean of the School of Religious Education was not as prestigious, perhaps, as being president, but surely, he felt, it was more worthwhile. Actually, he said, to be a teacher was more worthwhile than to be either dean or president: "A dean is a man who is too smart to be a president but not smart enough to remain a teacher!"

7
Missionary

On May 16, 1956, after 36 years of teaching, Dr. Dobbins retired from Southern Seminary. He might have remained at Southern as Senior Professor, but he wanted to leave Dr. Allen W. Graves, his choice as the second dean of the School of Religious Education, a free hand. Moreover, much to his dismay, for he loved the Seminary, conditions which led to the open break in faculty-administrative relations at Southern in 1958 were heating up. Since he felt that he could do little if he remained and he wanted to remain active and useful, it seemed wise to turn to another field of endeavor. (Perhaps this was the reason, suggests Dr. Oates, Letter, June 3, 1980, that he decided "not to discuss the issues in his classification of decades" in his 1967 article.) He was only sixty-nine. Since his mother had lived to be ninety-two, genetically he also might expect a number of years of useful life. What should one do when one retires? To Dr. Dobbins the answer to this question came as a response to prayer. Receiving a Macedonian call ("Help us"), he "retired" to teach at Golden Gate Seminary, California.

In January 1956, Dr. Harold K. Graves, the president of Golden Gate (brother of Dr. Allen Graves, dean at Southern), invited Dr. Dobbins to confer with the faculty of Golden Gate on "Problems of Curriculum Making." Earlier, in August 1955, at Glorieta Baptist Assembly, Dr. Dobbins had asked Dr. Graves if Golden Gate "might have use for him after he retired from Southern." Dr. Graves was delighted with the prospect. In fact, he says, he "urged him to move at once" (Letter, April 7, 1980). Since this seemed inadvisable, instead plans were worked out for Dr. Dobbins to move to California in 1956. In 1956 Golden Gate was seeking full accreditation from the American Association of Theological Schools. Since Dr. Dobbins had been instrumental in securing accreditation for the RE School at Southern, the faculty at Golden Gate felt that Dr. Dobbins' counsel would be helpful in securing accreditation for Golden Gate. In February he was invited by the trustees to join the faculty on a part-time basis as "Curriculum Consultant" and "Distinguished Professor of Church Administration." Initially Dr. Dobbins expected to stay at Golden Gate for two to three years at most. Instead he remained ten years, retiring a second time in 1966 at the age of seventy-nine. In 1942 he had voted against the admission of California to the Southern Baptist Convention. Now he recognized his mistake. Southern Baptist witness was essential if San Francisco (770,000 population), California (13,500,000), and the West (25,000,000) were to be won to Christ. Becoming a part of this witness, Dr. Dobbins made his ten years at Golden Gate the most productive years of his life.

Theoretically, at Golden Gate Dr. Dobbins taught only two classes each term. (Supposedly he was retired.) However, as he remarked before he left Louisville, "Retirement to inactivity has little appeal to a healthy man habited to work" (*Baptist Record,* March 9, 1956). True, at sixty-nine he no longer rose at 4:30 as he had when he was a boy; instead he awakened at 5:30-6:00, occasionally even remaining abed until 6:30. At three score and ten he recognized that the sun was setting, but oh, there was so much that needed to be done! "He must increase, but I must decrease" (John 3:30), perhaps the second most influential biblical passage in Dr. Dobbins' life, summarizes the thrust of the latter portion of his life. He had been saved to serve. Thus, although retired, he continued to work 12 hours a day. More accurately, he continued to enjoy life, for to Dr. Dobbins service for God was not work. It had been difficult to leave Louisville, where he and his wife had so many friends. But the West offered fresh, exciting opportunities for service. In the South, Southern Baptists were an established group. In California, Southern Baptists, who represented less than 1 percent of the population, tended to be regarded as being crude, narrow-minded, characteristics identified with their denominational label, *Southern* Baptists.

In Mill Valley, the location of the Seminary's new campus on Strawberry Point, in 1959 no Southern Baptist church existed. The Seminary family had to establish one. At first 49 members met in the Seminary chapel. Then, with help from churches in Texas and Georgia as well as a loan from the Home Mission Board, they were able to purchase a lot. In 1963, although few of the members had much money, they began to build. Dr. Dobbins was a charter member, occasional preacher, Adult Sunday School teacher, leader of Church Training, and funds-raiser. Wherever he went on his trips East (South), he spoke of the needs of the churches in the West. And he obtained money—from the churches of Roanoke, Virginia, as well as from other sources. Tiburon (Boulevard) Baptist Church occupied its building in September 1964.

"Watch the beginning of things," Dr. Boyce and Dr. Broadus used to say. Dr. Dobbins was fortunate enough to be at the beginning of things in California. In 1956 in population California was the fastest growing state in the West. Commenting on Dr. Dobbins' activities from 1956 to 1966, Dr. Harold Graves suggests that in his service at Golden Gate, Dr. Dobbins regarded himself as a missionary, a designation which Dr. Dobbins himself accepted. As a teacher-missionary, with his colleagues at the Seminary, Dr. Dobbins immediately involved himself in the life of the Bay Area, with its population of three to four millions—with fewer than 20 percent engaged in church work. Going wherever he was invited to go,

> to the little storefront churches, churches with limited facilities, to associational meetings, Sunday School Officers and Teachers' meetings, wherever there were those who would listen to his message, again and again he reiterated: A church is not an institution that has an educational program. It is an educational program (Allen Graves, "Eulogy for Gaines S. Dobbins," Southern Seminary, Tape, Sept. 27, 1978).

This was the message which he had presented successfully in Louisville. Would it work as well in the West, in San Francisco and Los Angeles, cities known for their sophistication and indifference? Of what value were methods of religious education and church administration in an urban society?

At first some of the California pastors questioned the validity of his approach. "Here, in California," he was told frankly, "your ideas simply won't work." Fortunately he was not required to endure a testing period as long as that which he had endured at Southern. Within a year the principles (principles, with methods being variable) which Dr. Dobbins advocated began to be accepted as being practical. What were these principles? Teach the Bible, advance the cause of missions, avoid controversy, "repackage" the presentation, witness to people where they are. Discover needs, respond to these needs, develop leadership. Involve people in the program of the church. In an urban society, Dr. Dobbins recognized, methods of presentation (packaging) required adaptation to fit the needs of the community; but, he insisted, regardless of whether a society is urban or rural, principles remain unchanged. Bible-based, person-centered witnessing produces results. To this approach, regardless of their sophistication, *people* will respond.

Of course, first they must be interested. (Interest leads to response.) In California, annual revivals seldom attracted crowds. Hour-long sermons certainly lacked appeal. To modern city dwellers, theological terminology frequently was meaningless. (To many even the language of the King James Version was strange.) The message of Christ, however, is not outmoded. If methods block witnessing, then why not change methods? If people will not come to the church, Dr. Dobbins suggested, why not take the church to the people?

> If apartment dwellers do not attend church services, why not arrange to have a chapel in the apartment complex to which residents will be invited? If the people of a neighborhood will not come to the church house to study the Bible, why not set up neighborhood Bible classes? If those who throng the city streets will not join a church group for discussion, why not provide a "coffee house" where they can engage in religious dialogue? If many who go to the motion picture will not go to church, why not secure use of the theater at an off-program time and stage an attractive religious service? If troubled people who need counseling will not go to the pastor, why not provide a Christian counseling center in an available place where they will come? When persons are known to have sickness, sorrow, bereavement, why not make an appointment to visit and take them Christian comfort? Where persons are confined—involuntarily or voluntarily—in prisons or hospitals or rest homes—why not make planned visits for personal helpfulness or group services? When there are neglected slum dwellers or underprivileged foreigner colonies, why not establish goodwill centers for their aid and uplift? Where people congregate in parks, why not mingle with them and give attractive gospel tracts to those who are receptive? When personal contacts are difficult, why not make tactful use of telephone for inquiry, religious conversation, invitation? Why not occasionally adjourn the regular church services to a needy unchurched area where under a tent or in some available building the services may be held? These and other possibilities unfold to the church in the city that catches the vision of taking Christ and the gospel to the people where they are ("The Christian Mission in Crisis," Ms., 1966).

The message of Christ is the most meaningful message in the world. This knowledge is of little value, however, Dr. Dobbins taught, unless it is accepted by people. This has always been true—whether the community is urban or rural. "Go ye into all the world . . . preach . . . teach . . . baptizing them," Christ's Commission, does not indicate that people will come to the church voluntarily; rather it indicates that it is the responsibility of the church to go to the people. First the church's message must appeal to those to whom it seeks to witness. "What will work in one community may be utterly impracticable in another" (*The Efficient Church,* 1923). Thus various methods may be—should be—used to present the Christian witness. People's needs and the message of Christ remain unchanged. Methods vary, however, according to the nature of the community.

Perhaps use of the word *methods* is misleading, for methods may include elements which are permanent or impermanent. Worship services, Bible study (Sunday School), and prayer sessions are aspects of methods which are permanent. Use of radio, television, sermons in song, and other methods (devices) of worship are aspects of methods which are impermanent. Sunday School may be held before or after the worship service. Prayer may be audible or silent, depending upon congregational needs. Techniques or approaches vary; principles should remain unchanged.

In a nation which, according to predictions, should be more than 80 percent urban in 1980, what methods should be taught to ministers whose congregations live in the cities? Since this was a question of education and administration, the faculty of Golden Gate turned to Dr. Dobbins for counsel. Answer to the question, he recognized, involved a rethinking of strategy, indeed, a determination of the reason for the Seminary's existence. In 1956 Golden Gate was still seeking to determine the means by which it could witness most effectively. Like pastor, like congregation. Humanly considered, the future of Southern Baptists in California (and the West) was linked directly to the type of leaders furnished by the Seminary. What should students at Golden Gate be taught?

Tentatively, at the end of his first year of teaching, Dr. Dobbins suggested that as its "distinctive contribution" Golden Gate should seek "ways of winning the people of the metropolis" (*Western Recorder,* April 11, 1957), a mission which was not being undertaken specifically by any of the other Southern Baptist seminaries. In 1959, having worked in the churches for three years, he addressed himself to the subject more explicitly. "Asked by the Trustees to speak to the question,

'What Is the Distinctive Mission of Golden Gate Seminary?' " he wrote, "I ventured to say that the peculiar mission of this child of the Southern Baptist Convention on the distant West Coast is to develop a new generation of ministers who can take the city for Christ" (*Watchman-Examiner*, Nov. 19, 1959).

Such a program was not to be entered into lightly, for, Dr. Dobbins warned, if Baptists lose themselves in "gadgetry," they will surely fail. On the one hand, he wrote, if Baptists cannot successfully adjust to an urban constituency, the denomination will perish. On the other hand,

If Baptists lose their essential character and mission in order to survive, they will as surely perish. How to maintain unaltered that which is divinely entrusted, yet propagate themselves by modern methods, is a challenge that must be met. . . . The education of the minister to meet this new urban challenge needs rethinking and reshaping. To the study of Bible, theology, history, homiletics, pastoral duties, Christian education—the "traditional disciplines"—must be added the intensive study of the city. Such study calls for clinical techniques, not just book courses in urban sociology.

Young ministers must be thrust into the stream of the city's life until they know it, understand it, weep over it, love it, feel its power and respond to its need. They must identify themselves with the city's constructive agencies and set themselves to purify it of evil and destructive influences. They must be utterly convinced that Christ and his gospel are the answer to the city's deepest need, yet equally convinced that the church must apply the answer to human situations (*Watchman-Examiner*, Nov. 19, 1959).

The statements in the article sound familiar. They represent an expansion of the ideas about which Dr. Dobbins had written in *The Efficient Church* (1923) and taught at Louisville and elsewhere for 39 years, yet they are different. In 1959 Dr. Dobbins regarded clinical training in urban problems as being essential in ministerial education. In 1920 he had regarded pastoral duties and Christian education as essential subjects. In advocating a shift of emphasis he did not suggest that courses in the now traditional disciplines be replaced with courses in urban problems. Rather, in 1959, Dr. Dobbins emphasized that pastoral duties and Christian education (Church Administration and Religious Education) included urbanology. Earlier, as a student in Chicago and New York in 1930, he wrote, "I foresaw that in my lifetime the city would become dominant and the churches would have to adjust to a new environment" (Biography III, *c.*1971). In 1930, however, since the rural and urban populations of the United States were almost equal, urbanology did not require separate study. By 1960 the urban figure had increased to 70 percent. In California the percentage had risen to 91 percent! With changes in the nature and the needs of the community, particularly in the West, in 1959 Dr. Dobbins recognized that nontraditional courses of study again were required. In an urban society—indeed, in an urban world, Baptists either must change their methods or perish.

These were (are) strong words, but Dr. Dobbins was not alone in his point of view. In 1964, addressing the Golden Gate faculty and trustees, Dr. Grady Cothen, then Executive-Secretary of the California Convention, challenged the Seminary to become "a laboratory to learn how to present Christ effectively to the cities" (*Encyclopedia of Southern Baptists,* 1971, III, 1739). The proposal was accepted by Dr. Harold K. Graves, the president, who appointed Dr. Dobbins head of a one-year study of the project. In 1966, following an 18-page report and recommendations by the faculty, Dr. Francis M. Dubose, superintendent of missions in Detroit, was asked to join Golden Gate as professor of a newly established department of missions and evangelism. Under Dr. Dubose, the combination of disciplines strongly emphasized the urban scene. Later the department was divided into two departments, with missions and the urban church being emphasized in one and evangelism and church development being emphasized in the other. "Both areas," states Dr. Graves, "bear the imprint of Dr. Dobbins' influence." In its "Urban Program" Golden Gate found its unifying purpose: In the name of Christ to respond to the spiritual hunger of all, but particularly to that of the teeming multitudes of the cities.

In 1978 Dr. Allen Graves suggested that much of the curriculum of Southern Seminary was initiated by Gaines Dobbins. A similar statement applies to Dr. Dobbins' influence upon the curriculum of Golden Gate Seminary. Yet the effect of Dr. Dobbins upon Southern Baptist educational practices extended far beyond his influence upon the seminaries. Directly and indirectly, through his lectures at Ridgecrest and Glorieta, his conferences in the churches, and as the result of his writing and teaching, he influenced some 10 million Baptists. Throughout the denomination his ideas changed the educational practices of the churches in the Southern Baptist Convention. In 1955, affecting Baptists in 19 countries outside the United States, Dr. Dobbins' educational influence became worldwide in scope. In 1955, at the Baptist World Alliance meeting in London, Dr. Dobbins, with Dr. Benjamin P. Browne initially as co-chairman, was instrumental in organizing what became known as the "Commission on Bible Teaching and Membership Training," an agency which influenced the educational activities of perhaps an additional half million to a million Baptists. "Bible Teaching and Training," a cumbersome term, is a near synonym for Sunday School, a designation less acceptable to European Baptists than "Bible Teaching and Training." As chairman of the Commission, from 1955 to 1965 Dr. Dobbins attended meetings held in London (1955), Washington (1956, 1961), Hong Kong (1957), Rüschlikon (1958), Rochester (1959), Rio (1960), Oslo (1962), Waco (1963), Hamburg (1964), and Miami Beach (1965). Although he retained membership on the Commission until 1975, Dr. Dobbins resigned as chairman in 1966.

Under the direction of Dr. Dobbins and Dr. Browne, the Commission on Bible Teaching had one major function: to promote "advance in Bible study and membership training in all areas of Baptist World Fellowship, especially through the teaching ministries of the churches." From 1905, the year in which the Baptist World Alliance was founded, to 1957, membership in Southern Baptist churches increased from 1,900,000 to 9,000,000, a growth of almost 400 percent. In 1905 European Baptists numbered 500,000; in 1957, 1,200,000, an increase of almost 150 percent. Why should Southern Baptists have had an increase more than twice that of their European brethren? This question the Commission sought to answer. Numbers, of course, are not the only measure of success. Nevertheless, numbers are significant.

To Dr. Dobbins as well as to the Commission, the primary cause or "secret" of Southern Baptist growth was Bible teaching and training, for adults as well as for young people and children. In many ways in 1957 the pattern of church life in churches outside the United States was that of Baptist churches in the South in 1905. Bible school was for children, teaching was by class rather than by department, ministers felt that they were preachers, not teachers. But something happened. Emphasizing tested methods of Bible study, Southern Baptists began to win multitudes to Christ. What were these methods? In 1963, at Waco, Dr. Dobbins proposed five constants:

1. Those to be enrolled should be located. First are members of a given church and their families. The most immediate "prospects" are those of the household of faith. Beyond these are friends, acquaintances, neighbors, fellow workers, who are not engaged in Bible study and who should be interested.

2. Time and place should be determined. The time should be suitable for the largest number of families. Many churches have found the best time to be the hour preceding the morning Sunday worship service. The place will ordinarily be a church building sufficiently large and adequately equipped to accommodate those who constitute legitimate prospects for enrolment.

3. Officers and teachers should be selected and trained. A rule of thumb is that one worker must be provided for every ten persons to be enrolled. The teacher is not a lecturer but identifies himself with the group and leads in Bible study.

4. Invitation to attend should be extended through personal contacts and visits. Sometimes the invitation will be preceded by friendly visits that win confidence, arouse interest, and excite desire for participation in Bible study.

5. Classes or departments should consist of persons of congenial ages. Children three years of age and under can best be cared for in a church nursery; children ages four and five can be better taught if they are separated from the children six to eight; the needs of the junior high school age can be met better if they are separated from those of senior high age. Young people have interests that are different from those of adults; men and women take part more readily in Bible study if they are in separate classes. Those who cannot attend the Sunday sessions should be enlisted in Bible study through an extension department that especially promotes Christian home life ("Go . . . Teach . . . All Nations," Position Paper, Waco, Aug. 1963).

These constants—earlier enumerated by Arthur Flake—summarize the principles of Sunday School administration which, after 43 years of experience, Dr. Dobbins regarded as being essential. They are principles which work—regardless of whether a church is located in Louisville, San Francisco, London, Capetown, Tokyo, or Rio. To disseminate this concept, which was largely unrecognized outside the United States, Dr. Dobbins obtained the names of 525 Baptist leaders responsible for religious education in 60 of the Alliance countries, a considerable undertaking in itself. Before 1956 no list of world Baptist educational leaders existed. Among this list of leaders, Dr. Dobbins circulated 7 Newsletters (1961-65), 7-25 pages in length, which included information concerning religious education and, of course, a questionnaire which sought to determine Baptist opinion. How practical, he asked, are the principles which the Commission on Bible Teaching is attempting to promote? The responses and Dr. Dobbins' responses to the responses are interesting.

Objection: The Sunday School has been and is properly a children's affair. It is not expected that adults continue in school.

Reply: The study of the Bible is a lifelong matter; adults need the Bible, are capable of learning, and will profit from its study fully as much as children.

Objection: Sunday for most adults is a day of rest and recreation. They may go to a morning worship service but they will not ordinarily attend a teaching service also.

Reply: Sunday is the Lord's day, divinely provided for human welfare, and the best rest and recreation come from the fellowship of Bible study in a congenial group. It is conclusive to say that in some parts of the Baptist world millions of adults do attend both teaching and preaching services.

Objection: The Sunday School may be a hindrance to the church's real function, namely, to lead the lost to a saving experience of Jesus Christ and to nurture them in this implanted life.

Reply: Admittedly, this may be a danger. Yet the Holy Spirit can and does use human agency and Bible knowledge to bring the lost to Christ and to develop the saved into soul-winning Christians.

Objection: Adults can best be taught by the minister from the pulpit. The minister is usually better qualified than lay members for this responsibility. Adults prefer to listen to him than to one of their own members.

Reply: Group Bible study, with active participation, is essential to permanent learning. Preaching is reinforced when accompanied by classroom teaching.

Objection: Many small churches do not have members who are capable of serving as officers and teachers.

Reply: Christians are disciples (learners) and can be taught. Jesus took a dozen untrained men and developed them. Patience is required but results will be assured. What better service can a pastor render than to find and teach selected church members to teach? ("Go . . . Teach . . . All Nations," 1963).

How win people to Christ? To this question, the Commission on Bible Teaching replied, simply: By teaching the Bible. To whom? To everyone, not just children, as was customary in most sections of the world, but to everyone, young and old alike. Teaching should be biblically based, democratically presented, evangelistic, and led by trained leaders. Literature should be attractively printed. Buildings should be well-equipped. Sound educational principles should be observed. Each of these aspects of witnessing is important, but most important is recognition of the church as an educational institution which seeks to teach the Bible to people wherever they gather, whenever they gather.

In June 1965, at the meeting of the Baptist World Alliance at Miami Beach, the Commission on Bible Teaching held its most successful meeting. Led by Dr. Dobbins, who now was seventy-eight, 93 participants from 30 countries (7 from Africa, 12 from Asia, 45 from North and South America, 26 from Europe, 3 from Australia) met to discuss common problems, to hear addresses, and to view a filmstrip on the subject of the witnessing church. In 1960, at Rio, participants from 17 countries had attended. Aside from providing fellowship, an accomplishment of considerable value, what did the meeting (a workshop) accomplish? Tangibly the Commission achieved—or at least laid the groundwork for achieving—three goals. Baptist leaders from 30 countries agreed: (1) That the church is more than simply a preaching point. (2) That Bible (Sunday) Schools should be provided for all ages, from children through adults, with methods varying according to the needs of the churches. And (3) That there was need for effective organization, literature, equipment, training, and further planning.

In 1965, for people as independent as Baptists, recognition of the function of the church as an educational agency represented a considerable step forward. To Dr. Dobbins, however, arousal of interest was only a first step. Agreement by 90 to 500 leaders did not constitute "grass roots" approval by local pastors or native leaders. Thus, from 1958 through 1964, as chairman of the Commission on Bible Teaching, Dr. Dobbins sought to establish support for the concept of the "All-Age" Bible School on the local level. He had been a missionary to California. For six years he became a missionary to the world, first as a missionary-advisor, in Europe (May-Sept. 1958), South America (June-July 1960), Canada (May-June 1961), Africa (Feb.-March 1962), and the Orient (June-Aug. 1964), and second, as a missionary-teacher, at Rüschlikon Baptist Seminary, Zürich (Sept.-Dec. 1958), Istituto Filadelfia, Rivoli (Jan. 1962), and Nigerian Baptist Seminary, Ogbomosho (April-May 1962).

At first Dr. Dobbins' proposals (as usual) were met with skepticism. In his travels, he wrote, repeatedly he met with the objection:

"But this is American with the label 'Made in America.' It won't work here!" "This is England, not the United States." Others joined in the chorus, substituting France, Italy, Spain, Switzerland, Germany, the Netherlands, South America, for England.

"Not so!" I replied. "What we are doing goes back to the original New Testament pattern of the teaching church. If we Southern Baptists deserve any credit, it is simply that, following our commitment to the New Testament as a sufficient guide, we have applied the example of Jesus and the disciples to the growing of churches as well as to doctrinal beliefs."

Evidences beyond America abound. Take Italy and Brazil, for examples. Both are almost solidly Roman Catholic. Southern Baptists have had missionaries in each country about the same length of time. In Italy the Sunday School has been primarily for children, the buildings one-room structures mainly for preaching. After 90 years, there are fewer than 5,000 Baptist church members in 120 churches and missions. By contrast, in Brazil, where the all-age Sunday School has been promoted from the beginning, there are more than 170,000 church members in more than 5,000 churches and missions. . . .

Consider Nigeria. When the Nigerian convention met at Ogbomosho recently [1962], an entire session was given to advance in Bible teaching and membership training. Within a little more than a century, starting from nothing, Baptist churches have come to number more than 1,000, with 60,000 members, and baptisms at the rate of 7,000 a year (*Western Recorder,* Jan. 17, 1957; "Rethinking the Strategy of World Missions," Speech, Golden Gate Seminary, Jan. 1963).

Skepticism, particularly skepticism directed against "things American," is difficult to overcome. Avoiding controversy, therefore, instead Dr. Dobbins presented his message patiently and simply: Training of children in Bible study is essential. Throughout his ministry Dr. Dobbins insisted that children should be given the best in equipment and facilities a church can offer. But adults also need training. "Growing, effective New Testament churches are built around people [adults as well as children] who know God's word and are trained to serve productively as church members." In Zürich a Dutch student summarized the reaction of his classmates to Dr. Dobbins' thesis:

The whole classs had a terrible time with that man. We thought he was forcing American ideas on us, and we were not very nice to him. But he was such a Christian, and so patient, we learned to love him (*Baptist Training Union Magazine,* Oct. 1966).

Europeans were not willing to accept "American ideas" without careful scrutiny. However, they responded to Dr. Dobbins' love for people and the biblical nature of his ideas. They appreciated his refusal to be dogmatic. Principles remain the same, he taught, but methods may vary depending upon local situations. At Zürich, Rivoli, Ogbomosho, and elsewhere, Dr. Dobbins overcame skepticism perhaps the only way it can be overcome, through biblical teaching, Christian love, and patience. In Nigeria, the students (local pastors) again were skeptical. "Praying about their reaction," said Dr. Dobbins,

I hit upon a plan. I would tell them of my conversion experience, my call to the ministry, and some of my problems of adjustment. They listened attentively and their emotions were stirred. "Now," I explained, "I want each of you to share with me and one another your Christian experience—your family background, your conversion experience, your call to the ministry, and your problems and difficulties. Write it briefly to be read and we'll give the next two or three class periods to this sharing.

The result was a deeply moving participation. Then the miracle for which I had been praying occurred: Jesus became one of the group, his promised presence literally felt. Suddenly there was no difference between these black students and my white lads back home. From that time forward I was one of them—and when my wife and I left, they and other students followed our car, as we drove away, singing a native song of farewell and crying out, "Goodbye and God bless you!"

We had come to belong to the community of the Loyal (Speech, "Let's Listen to What God Is Saying," Inter-Racial Conference, Selma, Ala., March 1, 1968).

"No one has ever come to our seminary who was better accepted. Nor have we ever had anyone who worked harder," wrote Dr. J. C. Pool, president of the Seminary (*California Southern Baptist*, July 5, 1962). As a parting gift the Seminary gave him a Scroll of Honor. The students presented him with the robes of a Yoruba chief.

In his travels as missionary-advisor and missionary-teacher, Dr. Dobbins emphasized a single theme: "Principles are not limited by geography," a statement which in phrasing he attributed to Dr. James L. Sullivan (*Baptist Program*, Feb. 1958). Adults will go to Sunday School—provided the Bible is made relevant and attractive enough to cause them to want to go. People will participate in Bible study and training—provided they share in the community of Christ's love. The concept of ministry, he said, must be enlarged to include an outreaching, encompassing understanding, and love of people.

Building on this foundation, Dr. Dobbins discovered that objections to Sunday Adult Bible study actually were not objections to Americanism. Rather they were objections based on tradition and dislike of change, objections which Americans themselves had made to Sunday Bible teaching half a century before and which he had discussed at length in his books (*Teaching Adults in the Sunday School,* 1936, *Meeting the Needs of Adults Through the Baptist Training Union,* 1947, *Understanding Adults,* 1948). In Europe, although a few adults might study the Bible at midweek services, tradition precluded Bible study for adults on Sunday. In Brazil, Nigeria, the United States, and other countries, experience demonstrated that a church can be more than a preaching point. Adults will participate in Bible training. Practice might argue otherwise. Experience showed that preaching complemented by Bible study produced a vibrant, witnessing church. In short, regardless of its location, in a church which is person centered,

> Teaching and preaching [are] like the two oars of a boat. If one oar only is used, the boat goes around in circles. If both oars are used, the boat goes forward. The evangelical advance for which we all pray and in which Baptists must have their worthy part awaits the realization and implementation of this truth. Teaching and preaching are correlatives in the winning of a lost world to Christ (*Baptist World,* Feb. 1964).

* * *

In May 1966, Dr. Dobbins resigned his position as chairman of the Commission on Bible Teaching and Training. In May, after having taught for ten years at Golden Gate Seminary, he began his "second retirement." Although he was almost eighty, he had been asked to remain at the Seminary, but Mrs. Dobbins' health was breaking and he recognized that it was time to move to Birmingham, where he might be close to his son and his family.

What should one do in one's second retirement? Rest, relax, enjoy life to the fullest? Only the third of these possibilities was possible for Gaines Dobbins. To serve God *is* to enjoy life to the fullest. In *The Years Ahead* (1959), three years after his first retirement he had written:

Jesus did not say, "Ye shall be witnesses unto me until you are sixty or seventy or eighty or ninety years of age"; he said, simply, "Ye shall be witnesses . . . " (Acts 1:8). In this greatest business in the world, there is no retirement age. When we enlisted as disciple-winners, it was for "the duration."

At the age of eighty Dr. Dobbins faced two possibilities, either to rust out or wear out. Like Paul, he chose to keep busy until he was called by the Lord. He no longer could walk "the hills and gullies" of Clinton or play golf as he once had been able (nine holes before getting the children off to school and going to the Seminary to teach). But he could care for his family, serve wherever he was called, and write. In Birmingham he had two granddaughters who would soon be teenagers and need counsel. And Mrs. Dobbins, who was confined to a nursing home in 1967, needed constant care. For eight hours each day for six years, lovingly and faithfully, Dr. Dobbins attended Mrs. Dobbins, and the other residents of the home as well. As spiritual director of South Haven, he was responsible for the chapel services which were held each afternoon. Usually he conducted the services himself. "These old folks" was a phrase he sometimes used to refer to the patients at the home. Although Dr. Dobbins was in his eighties, he did not think of himself as being old, for he wasn't.

Even a brief list of Dr. Dobbins' activities from 1966-78 is exhausting.

Vice-President, Western Religious Education Association, 1966; Member, Baptist World Alliance Commission on Bible Teaching and Membership Training, 1966-1975, Speaker, Einseideln (Switzerland), 1975; Visiting Lecturer, Samford University, Birmingham, Fall 1967; Boyce Bible School and Southern Seminary, Louisville, Fall 1975, 1976; Chaplain, South Haven Nursing Home, Birmingham, 1967-1973; Speaker, Southern Baptist Convention, 1972, 1977, 1978; Sunday School Teacher and Director of Leadership Training, Shades Mountain Baptist Church, Birmingham, 1969-1978; Author of 4 books, 3 tapes (Broadman), and 130 articles; Columnist, *The Alabama Baptist,* 1968-1978 (163 additional articles); spoke an average of four times a week, 1966-1978.

Obviously in his second retirement Dr. Dobbins did not dwell in the past. He used his memories, but he kept up with current thought by buying books and subscribing to current magazines (46 in 1978). "Make good wherever you are," Dr. Patterson had said, oh, so long ago. In

Birmingham, Dr. Dobbins again found a place of service. For 53 years he had been an ordained minister leading students and laymen in methods of worship and Bible study. In Birmingham he himself became a layman, serving his church, Shades Mountain, under the leadership of his pastor, Dr. Carl Giers and, later, Dr. Charles Carter.

What is a layman? Except to suggest that, according to New Testament practice, clergy and laity are scarcely distinguishable terms, apparently Dr. Dobbins did not try to define the word. In his actions he described its meaning. As a layman he daily visited the sick. On Sundays and weekdays he worked in the church, teaching Sunday School, conducting officers and teachers' meetings, holding training sessions for young people as well as adults. For a time, in the absence of a qualified staff member, he served unofficially as youth director. His thinking remained active and vigorous. At the age of eighty-three he was appointed director of leadership training, a position of considerable responsibility. This time the church furnished the "mimeograph." For his church Dr. Dobbins prepared literally hundreds of pages of outlines, lesson materials, guide sheets—whatever was necessary to train leaders to witness for Christ. *Good News to Change Lives* (1976), at least in part, was the published result. A friend was an alcoholic. His neighbor's daughter needed help. People needed counsel. As a layman ordained to service, he sought to apply the principles of pastoral care.

What is a layman? A layman is a person who seeks to "walk worthy of the Lord unto all pleasing, being fruitful in every good work, and increasing in the knowledge of God" (Col. 1:10). When he reached heaven, said Dr. Dobbins, perhaps God would give him a class to teach and then, at last, together with his friends he could learn the perfect will of God.

What does one do when one retires? Even though supposedly he was no longer active, to Dr. Dobbins came requests to conduct clinics in Alabama, West Virginia, and Missouri, to speak at conferences and conventions in Virginia, New Mexico, Kentucky, Louisiana, and Florida, to give counsel to committees studying problems of aging and of racial tension in Tennessee and Alabama. From pastors and missionaries he had met on his world tours came other requests. From Europe: Send us trained workers, pastors, teachers, administrators, translators who can help us with our work. From Asia, Africa, and South America: Send us missionaries, yes, but also, if only briefly, teachers, agriculturists, veterinarians, accountants, mechanics, architects, dentists, nurses, medical doctors—Christian lay people!

To these requests, using his feet while he was younger and sitting at his well-worn typewriter in his later years, Dr. Dobbins responded gladly. (He was happy, he said, that his difficulties started with his feet rather than with his head!) Now, now is the time to evangelize the world, he wrote.

> Never since Christ gave us his Commission until now has there been the practical possibility of evangelizing the world. Available to us now are radio, television, airplane, satellites, travel. Today there are almost no spots on earth that we cannot reach within 48 hours. Facing this, there is a rising demand on the part of adult Christians for participation in missions.
>
> The Southern Baptist slogan of the thirties, "The Evangelization of the World in Our Generation," was aborted by World War II and its aftermath. Bold Mission Thrust offers us a chance to begin anew (Unpublished ms., 1976-77).

"By the year 2001," stated Dr. Dobbins, "world population will have doubled, and a multiplied force of ordained clergy and appointed missionaries will be all but helpless in the face of insuperable difficulties of Christianizing the multiplied masses of unsaved." However, "with clergy and laity working together, the world can be reached for Christ . . ." (*Baptist World*, Feb. 1977). Thus, at the age of ninety-one, Dr. Dobbins enthusiastically supported the concept of a Missions Service Corps proposed by Baptists in 1975. It is a concept (the idea, not the title) which he had advocated throughout his career. "With clergy and laity working together, the world *can* be reached for Christ." The pastor is the leader, yet he is not the only leader. Both at home and abroad, effective witnessing requires use of the total resources of the church. This is the meaning of the Reformation. And, more significantly, this is the message of the New Testament.

* * *

While teaching a class in evangelism at Shades Mountain Baptist Church, writes Dr. Earl Kelly, I was interrupted by Dr. Dobbins, who apologized for arriving late. He had been on a speaking engagement away from Birmingham. Why was he late? Explained Dr. Dobbins:

> I tried to get here for the beginning of the class, but when I got off the bus the only taxi available was having trouble—the battery had run down and I had to wait. There was an old man of 65 driving the taxi. On the way to the church I

asked him, "Old man, how is it between you and Jesus?" He replied, "Not so good." I said to him, "There are not many days left to sunset. Wouldn't you like to have things right with Jesus before you die?"

Why was he late? While Dr. Kelly was teaching evangelism, Dr. Dobbins had been on the parking lot outside the church, leading the taxi driver to Christ.

Test the claims of John 7:17, Dr. Aven challenged his young student. Dr. Dobbins put the claims of Christ to the test. They work! They will work for anyone who puts Christ first. This was Dr. Dobbins' credo. The true value of a person's life lies not in his human accomplishments. True value lies in serving God.

8
1909-1978

In the preceding pages references have been made several times to "Dobbinology," the principal ideas which students and readers derived from Dr. Dobbins during the 69 years of his Christian ministry. Since Dr. Dobbins was a many faceted man, perhaps no two of his friends would select the same passages to illustrate his ideas. In 1976 Dr. Dobbins indicated 11 articles which he regarded as "the best" of the 160 articles which he wrote for *The Alabama Baptist* from 1968-76. In 1971 a number of Dr. Dobbins' former students suggested a variety of subjects, such as religious education, church administration, pastoral care, as areas from which copy should be reprinted. Unfortunately the selections were not specific enough to be of real value. In 1966 Dr. Philip B. Harris, editor of *The Baptist Training Union Magazine*, reprinted five extracts from Dr. Dobbins' writings. Excerpts from most of the passages suggested by Dr. Dobbins and Dr. Harris appear above and in the following pages. Otherwise, although helped by friends, I as biographer must bear responsibility for their selection.

Choice of excerpts has not been easy. Dr. Dobbins' writings are amazingly relevant, stimulating, and varied. Yet through the selections there runs a single theme: the lordship and saving power of Christ. To these selections should also be added passages from the earlier chapters of this book. Inclusively they should indicate the range of Dr. Dobbins' ideas and the reasons for his influence upon Southern Baptists during the past half century.

The Amazing Claims for Christ. There is superlative wisdom in John's beginning point. He begins where the issue centers—with the claims for Christ. He does not direct the attention to the reader or hearer himself, nor to the writer or speaker, but to a Person about whom the amazing claim is made that he is very God of very God who appears on the scene of history as a man as completely human as he is divine. This God-man he identifies as Jesus Christ, known personally to many among whom he lived. To this marvelous One John the Baptist had borne testimony that created widespread sensation as he declared him to be the long-expected Messiah. This divine-human Person, John declared, came through and to the Chosen People, many of whom rejected him; but to as many as received him, he gave the right to become children of God through faith in his name. In this Person was incarnated all the fullness of God. His forerunner, John the Baptist, declared himself to be of little importance in comparison with him of whom he bore witness. In contrast with the hope of salvation through keeping the law of Moses, Jesus Christ came to offer salvation to those who received it through no merit of their own. All that men need to know of God, they find in this unique One, divinely begotten and miraculously born.

So familiar are we with this amazing claim for Christ that it may have lost some of its power to startle, to grip attention, to break through the shell of egocentricity, and to lead to eager expectancy and to intense longing. But when the claim, with its striking originality and challenging implications, first dawns upon the consciousness of an intelligent seeker after truth and life, it possesses irresistible power to arrest attention. If this is *true,* it is the most important truth ever spoken. If it is *not* true, it disappoints the heart's deepest craving and plunges life back into confusion and despair. Could there be any better first sermon in a series of evangelistic meetings than . . . to start with John's startling picture of the Word made flesh who alone can give the right to become a child of God? *(Evangelism According to Christ,* 1949).

Testing the Claims. Ours is a scientific age. The scientist says, "Believe nothing that cannot be proved." The scientist, when asked if a thing is true, replies, "Try it out and see." Can the religion of Jesus Christ stand this test?

The scientific test is exactly what Jesus invites. To his first two disciples he said, "Come and see" (John 1:39). Again he said, "Ye shall know the truth, and the truth shall make you free" (John 8:32). Paul could fearlessly say, "Prove all things; hold fast that which is good" (1 Thess. 5:21). Christianity has absolutely nothing to fear from the true scientific spirit.

Science proposes to deal with facts. Christianity rests on historical facts. There are no better established facts in all history than the facts of the Bible. The Christian bases his certainty on the facts of experience. "I *know* whom I have believed" (2 Tim. 1:12), he can say with absolute assurance. Are not the facts of peace and joy and love and goodness as really facts as the facts of nature?

To one who doubts the power of God in Christ, we simply say, "Try it and see!" Turn in sincerity from the love of sin, take God at his word, accept and obey Christ as personal Saviour, and see what happens! Could any test be fairer? Could any proposition be more reasonable? There is a great deal of false science which claims that the material is the only form of reality; but a genuine and trustworthy science recognizes that there is reality in the spiritual as well as in the physical realm. We would bring all such honest thinkers face to face with Christ, that they may learn of him the way of life now and of life everlasting *(A Winning Witness,* 1938).

The Will of God. Certainly the highest purpose of the Christian should be to do the will of God. But the question constantly arises, "What is the will of God?" In the daily round of one's ordinary duties, how may one know whether or not he is doing God's will? Shall he depend upon his own judgment, or his conscience, or his desires, or the example of others? While these may sometimes be valuable indications, they can by no means be depended upon for sure and certain guidance. We must get back to something more solid and reliable. How know the will of God? Learn his will through a careful study of the Bible! There are of course many details, but Jesus summed it up in two great principles as stated in Luke 10:27: "Thou shalt love the Lord thy God with all thy heart, and with all thy soul, and with all thy strength, and with all thy mind; and thy neighbour as thyself." Here then is a simple, practical way to discover whether a given act is according to the will of God. "Does this show my love to God and my unselfish concern for others?" If what you are doing does not put first God and your fellows, you may rest assured that it is not according to his will *(Monthly B.Y.P.U. Magazine,* July 1929).

A Church. A church is truest to the New Testament ideal when it is regarded as a fellowship, a "beloved community" of regenerate persons. Those who constitute this *koinonia* are bound together by common faith and purpose; they seek not their own welfare but one another's; their experience with Christ impels them to share him with those outside their circle; the end of all their sacrifice and service is that Christ may be known and loved and obeyed by ever-increasing numbers "from Jerusalem unto the uttermost part." In this view the minister's chief role is that of leader or guide in the creation and development of this fellowship, in the confidence that all else can be easily made to follow if the church is a true spiritual community with Christ as its head *(Building Better Churches,* 1947).

Baptist Polity. Reduced to simplest possible statement, the essential principles to which Baptists hold with reference to their church polity may be thus summarized:

(1) As to the church, that it is local, independent, autonomous; (2) as to membership, that it should consist of baptized believers only; (3) as to government, that it is a pure democracy; (4) as to the ordinances, that they are symbols, or pictured truths; (5) as to cooperation, that it is voluntary, but fundamentally necessary; (6) as to fellowship, that it is based on common faith and a

voluntary covenant; (7) as to leadership, that it is called of God but elected by members of the body; (8) as to organization, that it must be true to New Testament principles, while utilizing all legitimate methods; (9) as to support, that it is the inescapable duty of every member, in proportion to ability; (10) as to authority, that the Bible, in its plain meaning as generally accepted by Baptists and interpreted by individual conscience, is sufficient and final *(Baptist Churches in Action,* 1929).

Service. The Christian is saved to serve. In the unselfish service of others he is most like his Master, and through this unselfish service the door is open for Christ to come into many hearts. The Christian who is always on the lookout for opportunities to help those in need, to minister to those who are sick, to comfort those who are in sorrow, and to do kindness to those whom he meets every day, will never be without opportunity to witness for Christ. Is it not strange that so many of us should have forgotten this ideal to which we committed ourselves when we accepted Christ? We need not expect our witness to be with power unless it is backed up by lives of unselfish service *(A Winning Witness,* 1938).

Success. The vast majority have never been able to possess physical and material guarantees. Only a few in any generation attain to a position of wealth and power, and even for these health fails, old age comes on, and no amount of property can buy off the Grim Reaper. The ancient pagan philosophy having broken down, is there no sure prescription for the Good Life?

Jesus replies with an emphatic "Yes!" The world has been looking for blessedness in exactly the opposite direction from which it is to be found. Over and over Jesus said, "He that findeth his life shall lose it: and he that loseth his life for my sake shall find it." (See Matt. 10:39; 16:25; Mark 8:35; Luke 9:24; 17:33; John 12:25.) Here is the heart of the Christian philosophy of life. Life, according to Jesus, is richest and fullest and at its best when it is being spent in self-forgetting service for his sake. Highest self-realization, in this revelation, comes through complete self-giving. Sacrifice means utter self-devotion to the will of God in Christ, the losing of oneself in the service of others for Christ's sake; but thus alone life comes to its fullest fruition. Living for self, saving one's life, seeking to get and keep and selfishly use the resources of life, means inevitable defeat and irreparable loss.

This principle holds good in every relationship of life. In business, in politics, in the home, in the school, in the community, the blessed people are those who give themselves in unselfish service for others in Christ's name. The unhappy, dissatisfied ones are the self-seekers whose lives grow more and more barren as they are increasingly absorbed in the pursuit of wealth and pleasure. Each of us can find demonstration in his own experience and observation of the truth of this Way of Life revealed by Jesus. Jesus himself lived this truth, literally losing his life to find it triumphantly and gloriously. If we would come after him, he tells us, we must deny self and take up our cross and follow him.

Herein lies the true meaning of life and the secret of successful living *(Deepening the Spiritual Life,* 1937).

Rank or Distinction. "Clergy" and "laity" are convenient distinctions which have little basis in New Testament teaching. Of course, there are distinctions of ability and devotion among church members, and some may be leaders while others are followers, but the "priesthood of all believers" forbids the exercise of lordship over the humblest member and opens the door of opportunity for the least to become the greatest. Democracy as conceived by the New Testament is more than a mode of government; it is a way of life. It makes reverence for personality normative in human relationships. It lights the candle of hope for the underprivileged and lays upon the privileged the burden of greater service. It repudiates all dictatorships, all totalitarianism, all coercion in the realm of things spiritual. It guarantees the "four freedoms." It is the star that guides humanity on its slow and tortuous way to the goal of the good life for all. In the nature of the case, the "beloved community" must be in the form of a spiritual democracy *(Building Better Churches,* 1947).

Evangelism. Turning to the eighth chapter of Acts, we find that Philip, the lay evangelist, went down to the city of Samaria and preached Christ to the people. Then we are told that "the people with one accord gave heed unto those things which Philip spake, hearing and seeing the miracles which he did" (Acts 8:6). The power of God came upon this good deacon who was witnessing so effectively for Christ, and many were converted. Devil-possessed minds were restored to sanity, the palsied and the lame were healed, "and there was great joy in that city."

Is not this the sort of revival that we need in thousands of communities throughout the South? Here was a godless people, a man who knew Christ and loved people, who went out into mission territory. The Samaritans were despised people, half-breed Jews, and were looked upon as ignorant and degraded. Yet this layman went into their midst and so witnessed for Christ that a multitude was won, and many were healed of their diseases. Is it not evident that we shall never win these lost multitudes if we depend on the preachers alone? There are not enough preachers to go around, and there are situations in which a good man or woman, not a preacher, can do more good than an ordained minister. Perhaps even now, Christ is saying to many of us, "Go, be my witnesses," and lost people out yonder somewhere are saying in their hearts, "Come over and help us." Why do we not heed their call? *(Baptist Adult Union Quarterly,* Aug. 1941).

Leadership. Examine this proposition: The typical Baptist church has in its membership as capable persons as the apostles were when Jesus first met them. He turned aside from the theologically and pedagogically trained rabbis, who were not teachable, and selected some plain working men (and later some women), apparently because they were willing and able to learn ("disciples"). Much of his redemptive ministry was devoted to getting these "unlettered" followers ready for the greatest leadership responsibility of history. His example and results amply justify the confidence that a church from its ranks can find and grow the leaders it needs *(The Sunday School Builder,* Jan. 1969).

The Ministry. Pastor-teacher is perhaps the best of all designations of the ministry of Jesus Christ. The two functions are inseparable—shepherding and teaching, teaching and shepherding. Practically all that Jesus did during his earthly ministry can be subsumed under this twofold activity. He made no sharp distinction between his teaching and his preaching. And his ministry of healing exemplified his shepherd heart. The pastor is called of God to be the representative of Jesus Christ. And how can he represent his Master if he does not follow his example? The pastor is called and commissioned to teach. . . .

The conception of a church closest to the mind of Christ is that of a school in Christian living. In this conception the pastor has a single track course. He is the God-called leader of a teaching institution. Preaching has its high place of proclamation and inspiration. Many helpers must be secured and trained. Efficient organization is necessary for the proper conduct of the school. Records and standards are needed as means of measuring strength and weakness. If the school is to grow, prospective members must be discovered and enrolled, and if a high level of attendance is to be maintained absentees must be visited. Comfort and counsel must be provided for those who are ill or in trouble. The winning of the lost to Christ must be kept uppermost as the supreme objective. The resources of the saved must be elicited, combined, and organized for all the purposes of Christ at home and abroad *(The Sunday School Builder,* Jan. 1946).

A Parable. Once upon a time a church called successively three members to serve on its staff. The first said: "Here I am; now your troubles are over. I will do everything that needs to be done." So he took over, coming to the church early and staying late, attending to an infinite multitude of details, relieving everyone else of all possible responsibility. But it came to pass that other staff members and the congregation grew weary of his super-industriousness and his job was given to another. The second said: "Here I am. You do the work while I do the planning and give the orders." And so he installed push buttons on his desk, announced changes, and publicized elaborate proposals, until the church was continuously astir with activity like unto a beehive. But again it came to pass that colleagues and congregation grew weary from overwork and exasperated from taking orders; so his place was declared vacant and given to another. The third said: "Here I am. Let us pray and plan and work together, that we may serve him who has chosen us and appointed us that we should go and bear fruit and that our fruit should abide." And the seeds which they sowed fell in good soil and brought forth abundantly *(A Ministering Church,* 1960).

Counseling. Today's pastor is an overburdened man. He must preach intelligently, feelingly, purposefully. With competitors for the time and attention of people which no other generation of preachers ever before faced, he must give unceasing time to the preparation of sermons and bring skill and artistry to their delivery. Innumerable calls are made on him for community and denominational service.

Demands must be met for the administration of the complex organizations of the church. Funerals, weddings, sick visitation, committee meetings, special occasions, and countless other services make a heavy drain on his time and energy. Yet if the shepherd of souls is true to the example of the Good Shepherd, he will not put anything ahead of the privilege of dealing face to face with those who need his personal counsel.

Such counseling is not amateur psychiatry. The psychiatrist is a highly specialized medical practitioner. The pastor may learn from him, but never is he to assume the psychiatrist's role. . . . [Nor does the minister] listen as a "father confessor" but as a man of God, as a representative of Jesus Christ, as a friend of this troubled friend who needs someone to share with him the burden. Always there must be the conscious realization that God, the patient and loving listener, will hear and help *(The Sunday School Builder,* July 1954).

Fear. Fear and anxiety have been and continue to be the lot of most people. Fear, the instinctive reaction to danger, is part of man's equipment for survival. If there were no fear in the presence of danger, not many of us would live long. There are life situations in which it is highly important to be troubled, worried, even anxious. Damage results when these responses become chronic and produce the mood of helplessness. The healthy-minded person does not try to avoid all situations of fear, worry, anxiety, but in these situations to find a constructive way out. Jesus did not say, "never worry," but rather, do not waste your energy in useless worry *(The Alabama Baptist,* Aug. 20, 1970).

Preaching. Tests of its effectiveness lie in the answer to this question: Has the message a dominant saving purpose, whatever the theme? "Saved" points in two directions: the renewed life of the believer and the saved life of the unbeliever. The evangelist proceeds on the assumption that "it is equally as important to save what we have as what we haven't," that church members who have fallen into sin have primary responsibility for restoring their relationship with God, since their backslidden condition is a hindrance to reaching the lost. The preacher's good news is that these Christians who have fallen by the wayside should be "set right . . . in a gentle way . . . by those who are spiritual . . . who may be tempted too" (Gal. 6:1, author's adaptation of TEV). Revival may have its most effective beginning when Christians in a state of inertia are revived. And the preaching most likely to reach them is not scathing denunciation but compassionate concern *(Good News to Change Lives,* 1976).

Compassion. Matthew describes a beautiful sunset scene in Capernaum. The news of the healing power of Jesus spread abroad, so that on this memorable evening the people came in great numbers, bringing the physically sick and the mentally ill, all of whom Jesus healed. Why did he do it? Seeking the answer, Matthew found it in the prophecy of Isaiah, "He himself took our illnesses and carried away our diseases." Jesus healed because he cared! "He had compassion on them." He suffered with them in their distress. He shared because he cared.

. . . The true level of Christian caring is found in the word which describes the caring of Jesus: *compassion.* The need of another becomes my need; the suffering of another brings me pain; the grief of another touches my heart with grief: the lostness of a soul without Christ brings a dark shadow over my soul *(The Alabama Baptist,* Oct. 5, 1972).

Passivity. It is saddening to realize how little originality most of us exhibit. We complacently accept conditions as they are, we lazily and uncritically adopt ideas handed down to us, we go our monotonous rounds doing "the same old thing in the same old way." Surely God must be dissatisfied with our lack of creativeness and our failure to use the constructive imagination with which he has endowed us *(Deepening the Spiritual Life,* 1937).

Administration. That administration is a detached fragment of the minister's total calling is a mistaken idea. Administration constitutes the circle of which other duties are related parts. Everything that the minister does of consequence is associated with the administrative function. This is made clear by Paul's choice of the word "bishop" to designate the man of God. It is not accidental that *episkopos*—bishop—should have been used in the only detailed description of the qualifications and duties of the man elsewhere called minister, pastor, elder, teacher, preacher, missionary, evangelist. It is customary to say that "bishop" is just another word for pastor and that every pastor is a bishop. But is there not a deeper reason for the use of the term? If we believe that Paul's words here as elsewhere carry the authority of inspiration, must we not believe that his use of *episkopos* is purposeful and significant?

The bishop's qualifications, both private and public, must be such as to fit him to "care for God's church" (1 Tim. 3:5). Everything that he is and does should be to the end that he may thus exercise this care. . . . The administrator, thus conceived, is primarily concerned with persons rather than with processes. Administration is of course concerned with organization and management, with efficiency and profits, with conservation and economy, but underlying all this is administration's basic concern for persons. There may be many immediate and instrumental aims, but the ultimate aim is enriched and growing personalities . . . . This viewpoint may well revolutionize the attitude of the minister toward his administrative duties.

A card on the pulpit stand, placed so that the preacher could not avoid seeing it, bore these words: "What are you trying to do to these people?" This question is equally pertinent in all administrative matters. The details of church life, the management of its affairs, the direction of its leaders, the cooperative solving of its problems are not machinery; they are the gospel on its behavioral side. In these ordinary affairs the minister sees human nature in action, he observes a democratic society given demonstration, he watches men and women grow under difficulties, he observes the impact of personality on personality, he studies the sources of conflict and their resolution. He finds out why and how persons can best work together. He realizes that in all these situations there are opportunities for communication of Christian truth fully as effective as preaching from the pulpit *(A Ministering Church,* 1960).

Methods. Truth is unchanging and Jesus Christ is "the same yesterday, today, and forever." Yet ways in which the biblical revelation and the living Word are presented change with changing times. The language of the King James Version of the Bible sounds strange and is even sometimes misleading to the modern city dweller. Theological terminology may have little or no significance to the urbanite. Methods of propagating the gospel and reaching the unreached which were successful in another environment and in another generation may be outmoded in today's city. This need of changed approach and media of communication is recognized by agencies that would sell their products and ideas to the city public. It must likewise be recognized by the church as the agent of Christianity if it is to fulfill its redemptive mission to the city. Vocabulary and methods are not sancrosanct and must be changed to meet changing needs. What these methods are can best be determined experimentally under the Holy Spirit's guidance ("The Christian Mission in Crisis," Ms., 1966).

Education. The best in educational theory and practice must be brought to the service of Christian education. A church's educational responsibility should no longer be considered that of fostering a number of more or less unrelated organizatons for teaching and training, but rather as that of maintaining an integrated and comprehensive educational program in the carrying out of which the several organizations are utilized *(The School in Which We Teach,* 1934).

Problems in Teaching. Religion being one of the most universally interesting subjects, why is it that much Bible teaching is dull and uninteresting? Assuredly, this is not the Bible's fault, for it is a book of fascinating human interest. Does not the answer often lie in the fact that the teacher sees little or no connection between the lesson and the life interests of those being taught? The result is that subject matter being presented seems remote from reality—something that happened long ago and far away. The class may listen respectfully, but since no responsive note is touched, they feel no call to take part, hence leave the class uninformed and uninspired.

An equally distressing mistake is sometimes made in an opposite direction. The teacher may choose a human interest theme, raise questions that arouse a response of keen interest, and engage the class in lively discussion; but all this may have little relation to the Bible lesson. Indeed, the discussion may become a debate in which nothing worth while is accomplished. Or the teacher may make a lecture or preach a sermon from which little, if any, knowledge of the Bible will be carried away by the class. The religious teacher accomplishes his purpose best who knows the interests of the members of his class, who also knows how the Bible matches these interests, and who effectually brings the two together *(Understanding Adults,* 1948).

Enriching Teaching. Teaching is at its best when it grows out of life experiences which are utilized for the guidance and enrichment of present and future experiences. The test of teaching is learning, and who learns anything apart from experience? Not always does the learning come through one's own direct experience; but it must first have passed through someone's experience.

Try to imagine something taught or learned that is unrelated to experience! The mother may teach the child that fire burns, and the child may learn this truth without being burned; but somebody had to learn it through experience, and it is doubtful whether the child truly learns what "burn" means until it undergoes the experience. Experience means just that—something undergone and done, resulting in change that makes a difference. The stimulus may be a present fact, the record of a past event, the statement of an idea, the impact of a transforming truth. The response may be a physical act, or mental perception, or emotional stirring, or volitional determination, or all of these together. When the resultant is viewed, we say that the individual thus acted upon and reacting has "learned." So we conclude that where there is no stimulus (without or within), there is no reaction; and where there is no reacting, there is no learning *(Teacher,* June 1945).

The Art of Teaching. A machine has been developed that is said to do a better job than the personal teacher. . . . Granting that the machine may have merit in certain kinds of teaching, it has a fatal defect: it lacks personality. It may help the student to acquire certain facts and even skills, but it cannot deal with his personal problems. After the facts have been learned, the machine cannot tell the learner what to do with them. It may present the *what,* but it cannot deal with the *why.* It may give the right answers to a problem in mathematics, but it cannot give the right answer to a problem in the moral and spiritual realm. It may give guidance in physical science, but it cannot point the way to Christ and to Christian living.

What is said about the machine as teacher may also be said about a human teacher who performs mechanically—the teacher who reads what somebody has written about the lesson, or who merely asks printed questions about a Bible passage, or who memorizes what he has to say and recites it. The teacher is not a record player to be wound up during the week so as to sound forth on Sunday.

Teaching is communication of truth by means of personality *(Guiding Adults in Bible Study,* 1960).

Education and Evangelism. Evangelism and education are twin heartbeats of a New Testament church. Whatever we do, we must keep in mind that it is "all for evangelism." To fail to evangelize is to fail. If we are true to the New Testament pattern, we will precede evangelism with teaching and follow it with teaching. We are not saved by knowledge but salvation is not apart from knowledge. Jesus said, "And ye shall know the truth, and the turth shall make you free" (John 8:32) *(Building a Better Sunday School,* 1957).

Character. It is a law of the spiritual world that God works through human beings to reach human beings. The church's message must be incarnated in men and women who translate the language of Scripture into the language of life. The supreme goal of a church is, therefore, the growing of Christian character. Only through members who possess true Christian character can a church hope to share effectively in winning a lost world and establishing a Christian social order. Jesus did not have much to say about the church as an institution. His concern was for human life, for purity and strength of character, for enriched and developed personality, for a relationship with God and with one another that would ensure the abundant life *(Working Together in a Spiritual Democracy,* 1935).

Words. The dawn of personality appears when the infant begins to speak. Think of the millions of words a normal person will speak in the course of a lifetime! Think of the billions of words written, printed, broadcast in a single year! What becomes of them? Jesus warns that "on the Judgment Day everyone will have to give account of every useless word he has ever spoken (or written). Your words will be used to judge you . . ." (Matt. 12:36-37, TEV). Our words are a part of us and they constitute one of the most significant attributes of personality.

Is it then too fantastic to think that our words go ahead of us to be used as the building material of the houses in which we will live in the hereafter? What sort of houses will our words, sifted to their essentials, build for eternity? It's a sobering thought. What a hellish house some people will have built! What an unadorned, empty house some will have built! And what houses of usefulness and loveliness will be the reward awaiting some because of their "beautiful words, wonderful words of life." The judgment of which Jesus speaks may well be to live in the kind of houses built out of the words which have characterized our inner lives. The Proverb says, "As a man thinks in his heart, so is he," and thought expresses itself in words *(The Alabama Baptist,* May 11, 1972).

Permanence and Change. Herein lies our crucial need: how to distinguish between principle and method, the changeless and the changing. The Seventies confront us with vast and radical changes. To ignore these changes and to try to retain the pattern of methods of a past era would be to deny the presence and guidance of the living Christ. To make changes unwarranted by the New Testament would be to repudiate the wisdom and authority of the Founder. To steer a steadfast course between these two perils is to meet successfully the challenge of unparalleled need and opportunity in the momentous years ahead *(The Alabama Baptist,* April 16, 1970).

Conclusions. What do these experiences and a lifetime of observation say about creating and maintaining zest for learning and teaching?

(1) Every normal person in whom the craving has not atrophied or been crushed wants to learn and keep on learning. The craving is self-perpetuating—the more it is satisfied the more persistent it becomes.

(2) Education is more than schooling—it is a lifelong activity and is essential to the experience of zestful living. Learning is living and when learning ceases life goes stale.

(3) Learning and teaching thrive best in a community of learners and teachers. This "community" may be a kindergarten, an elementary public school, a high school, a college or university; or a club, a neighborhood center, a labor union chapter, an informal fellowship, a bridge party, or wherever else a group of likeminded persons gather with common interests. Togetherness tends to foster educative experiences.

(4) To be truly creative, learning and teaching must permit freedom of thought and speech. The springs of creativeness dry up in a tightly controlled situation.

(5) Learning and teaching flourish when related to life situations. Abstractions, expressed in abstruse language, may not only be difficult to understand but also hard to recall and apply.

(6) Learning and teaching have greater leading-on value when they develop skills in dealing with problems that grow out of previous situations. Education is not a closed but an open-ended process that never reaches "the end" but always signs off with "to be continued."

(7) Learning and teaching grow best in a soil of humility. True scholarship is not proud that its possessor knows so much but humble because there is always so much more to be learned.

(8) Learning and teaching are vitalized when learner and teacher identify. The educative process is hindered when there is a felt gap between student and

instructor and unblocked when each has the role of both learner and teacher.

(9) Learning and teaching are correlatives; like love and marriage, horse and carriage, "you can't have the one without the other." It is difficult really to know anything until it has been shared, i.e., communicated, taught.

(10) An indispensable ingredient of learning and teaching is zeal—enthusiasm, fervor, dedication to the truth being gained and shared. Half-heartedness in either learner or teacher is fatal to the success of either.

The reward of the learner is that he becomes a better teacher; and of the teacher is that the more learning he shares the more he has. I count it my highest encomium to have a former student say, "You helped me to learn, and so better to live and give" *(Zest for Living,* 1977).

Faith and Hope. And so for six years as the day ended and the shadows gathered I stood beside my Beloved's bed in the Nursing Home and said: "I must go now before Old Man Dark catches me. Good night—I'll see you in the morning." Then one day the darkness we call Death gathered, the light in her eyes grew dim and went out. I kissed her cold and voiceless lips and said, "Good night—I'll see you in the morning." The lifeless body lies in the grave and the voiceless lips are silent, but the real person has gone on a voyage and will be waiting at her destination for me to join her.

Can we believe it? Or is this hope of life after death just wishful thinking to ease the pain of parting? Groping for answer, Koheleth (Ecclesiastes, the Preacher) says in his despair: "For the fate of the sons of men and the fate of beasts is the same; as one dies, so dies the other. They all have the same breath, and man has no advantage over the beasts; for all is vanity. All go to one place; all are from the dust, and all turn to dust again" (Eccl. 3:19-20, RSV). Is this life all there is? If so, is it worth living? As the end approaches, does it fill with dread of what lies ahead? Or has the fear of death been conquered?

For the Christian, as death approaches it loses its dread. Paul states the dilemma: "For to me to live is Christ, and to die is gain. . . . Yet which I shall choose I cannot tell. I am hard pressed between the two. My desire is to depart and be with Christ, for that is far better. But to remain in the flesh is more necessary on your account" (Phil. 1:21-24, RSV). We covet this assurance; but how can we be so sure? Are there evidences from other sources than the Bible that support its clear claim of life after death? From my reading and reasoning I have gathered testimonies that make assurance doubly sure.

Nature points to new life that follows apparent death. A few weeks ago the dogwoods, the redbuds, the flowering crabapple, the rose bushes, the hydrangeas, the four-o'clocks were barren and lifeless, the lawn grass brown and seemingly dead. Now as I look out my window I see them all coming alive and soon they will be bearing their glorious testimony that "if winter comes, can spring to far behind?"—if death seems to have won, will not life eventually claim the victory? And if this is true in the natural sphere, must it not also be in the spiritual?

From the world of the inanimate comes the assurance of indestructibility. The scientists tell us that nothing that exists is ever really destroyed. We see something burn and say, "It is destroyed," but not so. It has been changed into its component elements—heat, ashes, gases. We see where once the ancient building stood, now decayed and scarcely a remnant is left. We say, "It no longer exists," but not so. Its parts have just been changed and absorbed into earth and air. We see the wreckage of an automobile or airplane and we say, "It is demolished," but not so. Its apparently useless parts may be recycled and converted to other uses. From these and scores of other examples we conclude that nothing which exists becomes non-existent. And if this is true of things must it not be true also of persons? If things continue their existence, if The Christ arose from the grave, can we not assuredly believe that man made in the divine image cannot be annihilated?

Then we reason: If God made all things to keep on existing, is it not logical to reason that personality, the unique watermark of man and that which represents the crown of the Creator's creation, must surely be imperishable? Imagine an architect and builder constructing his greatest building and on completing it blowing it to pieces. Imagine a painter painting his masterpiece and slashing the canvas to shreds. Imagine a sculptor completing his supreme artistic achievement and then smashing it with a sledgehammer. Such a one would be pronounced insane. And God is not crazy! When he made man, he put "eternity in his heart." He knew that sin would mar his masterpiece but he provided in Christ the means of restoration. Surely we cannot doubt that he who made man can remake him and thus assure him of life beyond this life that has in it the quality of eternity?

Transcending all these evidences of life after death is the unmistakable biblical revelation and demonstration. Since God is immortal, it follows that those created in his image are made to live forever. We read that early in the history of man "Enoch walked with God: and he was not; for God took him" (Gen. 5:24). David, sorrowing over the death of his child, cried: "I shall go to him, but he shall not return to me" (2 Sam. 12:23). Job looked forward confidently to his vindication, if not in this life then in the life to come. The word *forever*, applied to man's existence, occurs over and over in the Psalms. The prophets were given to see that life does not end with death. Witness this affirmation: "And many of them that sleep in the dust of the earth shall awake, some to everlasting life, and some to shame and everlasting contempt. And they that be wise shall shine as the brightness of the firmament; and they that turn many to righteousness as the stars for ever and ever" (Dan. 12:2-3).

More than all others, Jesus Christ "brought life and immortality to light through the gospel" (2 Tim. 1:10). Crowning his teaching and his miracles of raising the dead is his own resurrection, "the guarantee that those who sleep in death will also be raised" (1 Cor. 15:20, TEV). Revelation pictures heaven, the abode of the living saved, in language that beggars description. And Paul exultantly declares concerning the body laid away in the grave:

"What is sown is perishable, what is raised is imperishable. It is sown in dishonor, it is raised in glory. It is sown in weakness, it is raised in power. . . . It is sown a physical body, it is raised a spiritual body. . . . When the perishable puts on the imperishable, and the mortal puts on immortality, then shall come to pass the saying that is written:

> Death is swallowed up in victory.
> O Death, where is thy victory?
> O Death, where is thy sting?

"Therefore . . . be steadfast, immovable, always abounding in the work of the Lord, knowing that in the Lord, your labor is not in vain" (1 Cor. 15:42-44,54-55, 58, RSV).

And so, Dear Heart, good night—I'll see you in the morning! *(The Alabama Baptist,* March 22, 1973).

Eternity. To this question, What is worth while? we then have the sublimely simple answer. That alone is worth while which can be carried joyously into eternity. With this as the test, what shall we set our hearts upon? What shall we give up? How shall we live the remainder of the days which may be granted to us? The answer becomes simple and the way is made plain when we can say with Paul, "For me to live is Christ, and to die is gain" *(Deepening the Spiritual Life,* 1937).

Epilogue

On Friday, September 22, 1978, at the age of ninety-two, Dr. Dobbins died without suffering at his home in Birmingham, Alabama. On September 25 a Memorial Service, attended by over 1,000 friends, was held at Shades Mountain Baptist Church. Touching tributes to Dr. Dobbins were paid by Dr. Raymond Rigdon, Dr. Allen Graves, Dr. Findley Edge, Dr. Harold Graves, Dr. Wayne Oates, and Dr. Charles Carter. Each spoke on various aspects of Dr. Dobbins' life, of Dr. Dobbins as administrator, teacher, missionary, counsellor, friend, and witness for Christ.

The family sat listening to the roll of Dr. Dobbins' honors.

Editor, author . . . initiator of Seminary courses in Christian journalism, psychology of religion, pastoral care . . . "Mr. Religious Education," "Mr. Church Administration," "Mr. Southern Baptist," D.D. and LL.D., Mississippi College, 1918, 1947 . . . Scroll of Honor, Rüschlikon Seminary, 1958, Distinguished Service Scroll, Istituto Filadelfia, 1962, E. Y. Mullins Award for Distinguished Denominational Service, Southern Seminary, 1966, Southern Baptist Association of Clinical Pastoral Education Award, 1966, Emeritus Professor, Southern Seminary, 1968, Distinguished Service Award, Glorieta Assembly, 1969, Distinguished Service Award, American Protestant Hospital Association, College of Chaplains, 1972, Golden Arrow Award, Mississippi College, 1973, Distinguished Service Scroll, Alabama Baptist Historical Association, 1975, Gaines Dobbins Chair of Church Administration, Southern Seminary, 1976, Gaines Dobbins Music-Education Building, Shades Mountain Baptist Church, 1978.

Yes, the honors were rightly stated, the tributes sincere and *deeply* appreciated, but they presented only a picture in part. Other strokes of the brush were needed to complete the portrait—of Dr. Dobbins at Gloster, calling his firstborn son "Boy" (I wonder why?); at Lousiville, in a two-room apartment, swallowing his pride and hanging patched curtains given by a well-meaning friend to the preacher and his bride; at Nashville, being fussed at by Dr. Dargan for borrowing a book without permission (and later recognizing that Dr. Dargan was right); at Louisville, returning home saddened when one of the students performed poorly on his degree examination; at Columbia, performing the wedding ceremony for his son (and then, in Birmingham, some 30 years later, for his granddaughter); at Mill Valley, working in the garden with Mrs. Dobbins; at Birmingham, after his last stay in the hospital, saying cheerfully, with a twinkle in his eye, "I have discovered the Eleventh Beatitude. Blessed are the pacemakers!"

At the service, eight-year-old Joel Pate sat quietly, saying good-bye to his friend. He had asked his parents to let him miss school to attend the funeral because, he said, Dr. Dobbins always shook his hand and talked to him on Sunday mornings. His presence would have pleased Dr. Dobbins, for Dr. Dobbins enjoyed meeting people and making friends to the end of his life. To Dr. Dobbins, Joel was an individual, a person of infinite worth. Three years before he died, said Dr. Oates, Dr. Dobbins gave him a priceless piece of advice: "As young as you are, you need continually to make new friends. If I had relied entirely on the friends I had when I was young, I wouldn't have any friends now" (Memorial Service, Tape, Sept. 25, 1978). Dr. Dobbins' interest in others was genuine, and others responded with affection and appreciation. This had not always been the case. Through Christ he learned to love and value people . . . to become person-minded. Joel was his friend.

Yet even these glimpses inadequately capture Dr. Dobbins' personality. Nor is it presented adequately in the pages of this book. Perhaps the clearest portrait of Dr. Dobbins is expressed in his own words, in *Zest for Living* (1977):

Those who have somehow managed to come to length of years no doubt have turning points in their lives and wonder why certain pivotal events transpired. Was it just happen-so or was there a pattern that allowed for human freedom but also indicated a Designer working out a more or less predetermined design?

. . . Why did my father move from the farm to town? Why did he become a hotel keeper? Certainly not just in order that I might be given opportunities I could not have known in the village where I grew up. Life was changed for the whole family and we all benefited. Yet my experiences were such as to make me now see that a Power behind the scenes was at work getting me ready for an unanticipated future.

Why did my brother have to die? Certainly not that by his tragic death I might be blessed. But since his untimely death disrupted his plans to be a minister, may not an all-seeing Eye have foreseen in me a possible replacement?

Why did I become an apprentice printer? It might seem merely accidental, but would it be incredible fatalism to posit a wise Providence introducing me to a career in which I would find my aptitudes and ambitions eventually fulfilled?

Why were my father and my family led to move to [McHenry]? . . . Why did I pie the type just before returning home, thus having to stay a couple of weeks longer? . . Why was I moved, almost against my will, to go to college and to choose a Christian school?

Each of these questions is part of a larger question: Is there purpose in life? This question, stated Dr. Dobbins, cannot be answered satisfactorily except by a Christian. As Browning wrote, "Our times are in his hand/Who saith, 'A whole I planned' " ("Rabbi Ben Ezra"), or better, as Paul concluded, "God did this according to his eternal purpose."

Dr. Dobbins was not a fatalist. As a boy, ambitiously *he* decided that he wanted to be more than "just a country jake." *He* was responsible for his decision to continue his education. Yet he was guided by an unseen power, a power which he could either accept or reject. Thus he could write that his "life, with limitless variations, may in a way be that of Everyman's." Following God's will, stumblingly yet purposefully, Everyman may live a life that is meaningful. To each individual Christ promises and provides—if his claims are accepted—the means by which each may reach his or her highest potential. With these words the sketch of Dr. Dobbins' life may be concluded. Dr. Dobbins was a man of purpose. To anyone who follows Christ, life has purpose, a purpose which can be accepted fully or in part. Dr. Dobbins chose acceptance. *Nunc dimittis.* The world is better for his choice.

Books by Gaines S. Dobbins

The Efficient Church. Nashville, Sunday School Board, 1923.

The Sunday School Manual, by B. W. Spilman and P. E. Burroughs, revised by Gaines S. Dobbins. Nashville, Sunday School Board, 1923.

Working with Intermediates. Nashville, Sunday School Board, 1926.

Outline of the History of Religious Education. Louisville, author, 1926.

Source Book in the History, Theory and Practice of Religious Education. Louisville, author, 1926.

Baptist Churches in Action. Nashville, Sunday School Board, 1929.

Edgar Young Mullins—A Study in Christian Character. Louisville, Southern Seminary, 1929.

How to Teach Young People and Adults in the Sunday School. Nashville, Sunday School Board, 1930.

Vitalizing the Church Program, with John L. Riffey. Nashville, Broadman Press, 1933. *Vitalizando el Programa de la Iglesia,* tr. Arturo Corugedo. El Paso, Casa Bautista de Publicaciones, 1950.

The School in Which We Teach. Nashville, Sunday School Board, 1934. *The Bible and the Bible School,* with J. B. Weatherspoon. Nashville, Broadman Press, 1935. Reprint (Part II) of *The School in Which We Teach*.

Working Together in a Spiritual Democracy. Nashville, Sunday School Board, 1935.

Teaching Adults in the Sunday School. Nashville, Broadman Press, 1936. *Ensenaňdo a los Adultos en la Escuela Dominical,* tr. A. E. Corugedo Biberia. El Paso, Casa Bautista de Publicaciones, 1957.

Deepening the Spiritual Life. Nashville, Sunday School Board, 1937. *Crescei na Graça,* tr. Gerson Rocha. Rio de Janeiro, Casa Publicadora Batista, 1951, 1967.

A Winning Witness. Nashville, Sunday School Board, 1938.

Can a Religious Democracy Survive? New York, Revell, 1941.

The Improvement of Teaching in the Sunday School. Nashville, Sunday School Board, 1943. *Melhor Ensino na Escola Dominical*. Rio de Janerio,

Casa Publicadora Batista, 1960. *The Improvement of Teaching in the Sunday School.* Nashville, Convention Press, 1973, a rewriting of the 1943 text.

Enlisting for Christ Our Returned Servicemen. Nashville, Sunday School Board, 1945.

Meeting the Needs of Adults Through the Baptist Training Union. Nashville, Sunday School Board, 1947.

Building Better Churches: A Guide to the Pastoral Ministry. Nashville, Broadman Press, 1947. Published in a Chinese edition, 1963.

Understanding Adults. Nashville, Broadman Press, 1948.

Evangelism According to Christ. Nashville, Broadman Press, 1949; first ed., Harper, 1949.

The Churchbook: A Treasury of Materials and Methods. Nashville, Broadman Press, 1951. Translated by John Lee and published in a Korean edition, 1970.

Winning the Children. Nashville, Broadman Press, 1953.

Building a Better Sunday School Through the Weekly Officers and Teachers' Meeting. Nashville, Convention Press, 1957.

The Years Ahead. Nashville, Convention Press, 1959.

Guiding Adults in Bible Study. Nashville, Convention Press, 1960.

A Ministering Church. Nashville, Broadman Press, 1960.

The Church at Worship. Nashville, Broadman Press, 1962.

Great Teachers Make a Difference. Nashville, Broadman Press, 1965.

Learning to Lead. Nashville, Broadman Press, 1968.

Good News to Change Lives: Evangelism for an age of uncertainty. Nashville, Broadman Press, 1976.

Zest for Living. Waco, Texas, Word Books, 1977.